EIGHT BULLETS

E·I·G·H·T
BULLETS

One Woman's Story of Surviving Anti-Gay Violence

by CLAUDIA BRENNER
with HANNAH ASHLEY

Firebrand
Books

Selections from this book, in earlier versions, appeared in *Femicide: The Politics of Woman Hating* by Diana E. H. Russell, and *Hate Crimes: Confronting Violence Against Lesbians and Gay Men*, edited by Kevin T. Berrill and Gregory M. Herek.

Book and cover design by Nightwood Design

Printed in the United States on acid-free paper by McNaughton & Gunn

10 9 8 7 6 5 4 3 2 1

Library of Congress Cataloging-in-Publication Data

Brenner, Claudia, 1956–
    Eight bullets : one woman's story of surviving anti-gay violence / by Claudia Brenner with Hannah Ashley.
        p.   cm.
    ISBN 1-56341-055-9 — ISBN 1-56341-056-7 (paper)
    1. Lesbians—Crimes against—United States. 2. Lesbians—Crimes against—Pennsylvania.   I. Ashley, Hannah, 1969– . II. Title.
HV6250.4.H66B74   1995
364.1'523'092—dc20
[B]   95-4327
                                                                          CIP

˒ ACKNOWLEDGMENTS ˒

Thanks to Nancy Bereano for supporting this book throughout. And to my many friends for making this project a priority in their busy lives—remembering, reading, and making suggestions: Karen, Kris, Gina, Satya, Rhoda, Linda, Evelyn, Chris, Kevin, Andrea, Jill, and especially Anne, who at times cared more about this book than I did. May this book be a tool to help eliminate the fear and the hatred in our lives.

Claudia Brenner

I would like to thank my family for supporting me in being a writer and a lesbian, the Dinner Collective for their encouragement, Anndee and Alexis for their comments on the manuscript, Toba for loving and listening to me, and Claudia for asking me one Shabbat dinner to write a book with her.

Hannah Ashley

For Rebecca Wight

October 17, 1959–May 13, 1988

*"I only hope that heaven is not so big a place that
we can't find each other..." (From the AIDS Quilt
panel for Charles Catine)*

Most survivors seek the resolution of their traumatic experience within the confines of their personal lives. But a significant minority, as a result of the trauma, feel called upon to engage in a wider world. These survivors recognize a political or religious dimension in their misfortune and discover that they can transform the meaning of their personal tragedy by making it the basis for social action.

Judith Herman, *Trauma and Recovery*

ꞏ PROLOGUE ꞏ

DEAD WOMAN'S HOLLOW ROAD

Claudia: This is the map. This is the same map that Rebecca and I had. Think I'm talking loud enough?
Jill: I think so. Do you want to move the mike closer?
C: No, that's okay. (Sigh.) It's so scary with all the decisions that we made that led up to Rebecca being killed. It's so weird talking... thinking about it; it all made sense at the time. Like the reason that we met at Michaux State Forest was because there was a park there where we had met once before. It's just about halfway between Ithaca [New York] and Blacksburg [Virginia]. It was nice to meet halfway.

We had slept in the campground of the park. See? This is Pine Grove Furnace State Park. And here's the Appalachian Trail that runs through it. That's the yellow.

After the last time, Rebecca said sleeping in a tent in a campground was like sleeping in a parking lot. So when we were making plans the week before for this trip, she looked on the map and said, "Why don't we go on the Appalachian Trail?" So we decided to meet at the area we both knew, at the headquarters of the campground, and then hike. And that's where we met, that part of the forest, probably out here, off the map.

I can't show you where it is.

This is where we parked the car. Dead Woman's Hollow Road. That's where we parked the fucking car.

J: That's the name of the road?

C: Dead Woman's Hollow Road. The reason it's called that...Denny Beaver told me. He found out. He knew it was weird.

He said that in 1917 a woman got bit by a rattlesnake up there, and it took them three days to find her. She died. And that's why they call it Dead Woman's Hollow Road. And that's where we parked the car. We didn't know it was called that at the time. We had seen it on the map, we saw that it was called that, and...well, I'll go back, I'll try to tell the story chronologically.

We saw that road, Dead Woman's Hollow and Blueberry Hollow Road, and we talked about picking blueberries. We knew it was the wrong time of year, but I was telling her how fun it was to go to Maine in August and pick blueberries.

And Dead Woman's Hollow Road was the name of the road where we parked the car. That's one of the coincidences that makes the story sort of unbelievable.

So we met—it was May 12—on a Thursday afternoon. My truck was fucking up the whole way down there. I had to keep the heat and the fan on *High* because it was threatening to overheat. I was broiling.

J: Ugh.

C: I got there late, and so did she. We were supposed to meet at 4:30...I don't know. It was about 5:00. Ahhh.

So hard to do—to keep thinking. I have to, just to tell the story. I pulled my truck in, finally. I got all lost, can't remember what I did, some weirdness coming down. Instead of staying on 81 I went on some other road, a back way, and I got mixed up and I had to stop about five times for directions. Kept stopping and being worried about my truck, and broiling, not wanting to turn my truck off and wanting to turn my truck off. I was pretty fried after I got there. She had had trouble with her car, too. She had turned it on once during the trip and it wouldn't start, but then it did. I understood the trouble in my truck. Hers was a little more mysterious.

But she was there by the time I got there, and we were happy to see each other. Some people had given her a map just before they left. So we had an idea where we were. We had seen the Appalachian Trail before, and we knew it went through there, but we didn't have a lot of detailed information. She had gotten a map and we were happy about that, we had a good map. Ahhh. (Crying.) I guess it was good I had a good map.

It's weird to have the tape recorder on. But we're doing it for a reason.

J: Mm-hmm.

C: There were some men around when we first met. So we were kind of low key about hugging and kissing, but not very. They looked like workers. And later, much later—

When we figured out where we were going we took Rebecca's car and left my truck in the parking lot with a little note on the dashboard saying that we were on the Appalachian Trail and when we would be back.

Much later, when Heather and Sloan drove there to try and get my truck, it turned out that the workers were really, really nice people. They found where my truck was parked. Everyone knew that it was my truck, and they all said things to Heather and Sloan like how they were so, so sorry. "We just can't tell you how sorry we are." "It should never have happened." They worked there and they loved the park. It was theirs. Anyway, that was the truck.

So, Rebecca and I sat in the parking lot and tried to figure out where to go. She was good at reading topographical maps, and I can, too. She picked out...we were looking at where everything was in relationship to the roads and the views and fun things to do. She saw that there was a loop, called the Rocky Knob Trail, off of the Appalachian Trail, and she thought that that would make a really nice day hike.

We only had—we met Thursday and we had Thursday night, all day Friday and Friday night, and then on Saturday we were going to D.C., to Rebecca's sister's, to celebrate her sister's birthday. We would come back Sunday and spend the night around here and then go back, me north and her south, on Monday. So we didn't have a lot of time.

Rebecca thought we should hike in, set up camp somewhere along the Appalachian Trail, which turned out to be at Birch Run Shelters, sleep over, go for a day hike the next day, sleep over again. Then go back to the car and leave for her sister's. And that's where we thought we were leaving the car, by the three towers. So we got everything out of my truck and locked it up and drove to what we thought...where we thought we were going to be, right here by the forest fire towers. But there was no place to leave the car that was safe. See how there are parking places in other spots but not there? So without really knowing what we were doing we just drove up, and we saw a parking--see that little cross? That means parking.

We just parked there. Not really looking at the road sign, not paying attention to the name. And that's where we got both our packs out and repacked to make sure we had everything. I left some extra stuff in her car because it was pretty clear it wasn't going to rain, blahblahblah. I packed up and she packed up, and we got on the trail. I don't know. It was around 6:00 when we started walking south on the Appalachian Trail.

We walked past Shippensburg Road. There were some houses there, and across the road were trees, and then we walked through more woods to Birch Run Shelters. The last thing we had to do was cross a little stream, and we had fun there because I was scared. There was a series of small stones to step on, and that's always been hard for me, balancing on little things.

The water wasn't deep, but it was really cold. I told Rebecca not to look because I got self-conscious. She went across, and I did get self-conscious, but I did it anyway. It was easy.

So we were just...it wasn't fabulously beautiful, and it wasn't incredible, but it was nice and it was a nice walk. We got to the campsite. It wasn't a fabulous campsite. There were some lean-tos that we didn't really want to be in, and an outhouse. It was big. It looked like a whole Boy Scout troop could stay there. We found a place to put the tent up that was down a few notches topographically, and a little bit away from the lean-to, but still within the boundaries of the campsite. When you looked out of the tent, you had to stretch your head up to see the lean-to. We were acknowledging the fact that there was a campsite, but not really using it.

I remember Rebecca liked the campsites on the Appalachian Trail because they had logbooks where everyone signed in. She had been on the Appalachian Trail a lot. She called it the A.T.—that's what hip people call it. So during the whole first mile, mile and a half that we walked, we were talking about the A.T. She was telling me the history of it, how it got developed, how it was federal land, and how sometimes it got moved because it was on people's private property. It was interesting.

She said a lot of campsites had logbooks in the lean-tos, and, in fact, she was walking over toward the lean-to the next morning when she met—I don't know what to call him. Fuckhead. It appeals to me: F.H. She didn't know he was there. She was going to see if there was a logbook in the lean-to, and there wasn't any logbook there was only Stephen Roy Carr. She said there were logbooks and everyone would sign in. She was talking about really liking that and about how fun it was to find out who had been there. Sometimes they'd write little stories. It was fun.

Another fun thing that I remember about preparing for the trip was...you know how there are sleeping bags that zip together? Well, hers had a right-hand zipper. When she was in a relationship with this guy, he had the other half. So that week before, I was asking around for a left-handed bag so we could zip them together, and I never looked at my own sleeping bag until one or two days before. And it turned out I had a left-handed zipper on my sleeping bag! It was the first time I had been camping and sleeping with somebody in zipped-up bags. Incredible luxury.

When we got to the shelter, there was still plenty of light. There was nobody there, and it was nice. It wasn't fabulous but it was nice. We set up the tent, made dinner, didn't make a fire. Rebecca wasn't much into making fires because real campers don't make campfires, they just use their little stoves that run off camping fuel. She had said we could make one if I wanted to. She could get into it on the level of Fire: you know, fun—but not necessarily that that was *camping*. She had always gone on such rugged trips that as soon as it got dark all you wanted to do was crash out. That was the type of camping she was used to.

Anyway, I had a small stomachache all evening long, probably from eating meat, and the heat and stress on the trip down. So we went to bed a little while after it got dark.

We woke up pretty late the next morning. I left the tent first, I think, and then she did. It felt like we were totally alone. We went to the stream together and washed up, and then came back and were hanging out, outside of the tent. I started to make water for coffee and breakfast. I had to boil a lot of water. We were treating it because we weren't sure if it was good. Rebecca went up to use the outhouse. I remember watching her from behind and thinking that she was really hot. Meanwhile, I was just hanging out, waiting for the water to boil. A little while later, maybe ten minutes, she came back and said, "We're not alone here, Claude, we're not alone. We've got to put on our clothes."

J: It was warm?

C: Warm and sunny enough to be naked.

J: What time was it?

C: By then, mid-morning. At least 9:30 or 10:00. So she told me that, and I said, "What, what?" Not in a panic, but just, "What?" She said that she had gone from the outhouse toward the lean-to to see if there was a logbook there so that she could bring it back and we could read it while we were eating breakfast, and she came upon this...man.

She told me he was a creep. That was the first thing she told me. She was totally naked except for her sneakers. She said something like, "I'm embarrassed," or, "I'm really embarrassed, I thought we were alone"—meaning her and me. She was treating him as though he was another camper who would also be embarrassed but would probably think it's pretty normal to be naked in the woods when you think you're alone. She told me he said he had arrived late at night and thought he was the only one there. Which was confusing because later on it seemed like he might have seen us beforehand. Exactly like any number of...she surprised him as much as he surprised her.

I'm not sure. That's the impression I had, though, that up until that point he hadn't actually seen us. It might not be true.

J: Did he try to get close to her?

C: She said when he turned around he had a hard-on. We talked about how freaky that was, about how men didn't need to have hard-ons but how they had convinced themselves they had no control over their sexuality. We had a discussion about how some men were not like that, how our friend Jeff would have said he could have controlled it if he had a hard-on, but a lot of men say they can't control themselves. He saw a naked woman, he had a hard-on.

He asked her for cigarettes. She said she didn't have any, she didn't smoke. I think that was the end of the conversation. Then she came back to me and said, "We've got to put on our clothes." And she told me he was a creep.

We talked about him a little bit. She described him as the kind of guy who came into the woods because he had nothing to do and would lay around doing crossword puzzles. She said that. I never knew if she actually saw a crossword book, or if that was just some association she had in her head with creepy guys in the woods.

When I found out, much later, that he was a fugitive, it made sense that he didn't have any cigarettes. He was clearly an addicted smoker, and he was so fucked up that his basic needs included a pack of cigarettes and...he turned out to have committed a crime in Florida. Just, *just* grand larceny, and he skipped out on something. So it turned out that the impression he gave Rebecca made sense, somebody who had a lot of time to kill...her assessment was exactly accurate.

So she came back and we thought, *Fuck, this is a bummer, but what are you going to do?* I put on shorts and she put on long pants. We talked about that, that she hadn't brought shorts because I had kept telling her how cold it was in Ithaca. She had gotten the idea it was going to be really cold in Pennsylvania, too.

We ate breakfast and chatted. I was trying to find out why she didn't like oatmeal. I told her how Annie and Satya liked to eat oatmeal with maple syrup and how I didn't like that. She was putting a lot of raisins in hers.

For some reason, I had brought nutritional yeast and she was teasing me about what was I going to use it for. I didn't know. But it was light, so I brought it. I was telling her that I was bringing it to show her. Goofy. We were having fun together, just hanging around. No rush, no struggles, just being together and talking about all kinds of stuff, catching up.

It was fun. Not fabulous, just fun. It wasn't the greatest day of my life at all, but it was nice. Nice to be outside, nice that the sun was shining. It didn't really matter that there was this person. In fact, we had sort of lost track of him, just let him be. Assuming that he wanted to be let be and we wanted to be let be. That seemed normal. I still think it's normal. Sometimes a person wants to make friends with you, but if you don't want to, you don't have to.

Eventually, we got out the map again and talked about what we were going to do with the day. We had thought that we would leave the tent there, at the same site, and take a day hike, without our packs. The distance from Birch Run to the beginning of the Rocky Knob Trail is probably less than a mile, and then the trail itself is probably two to three miles, with all the curviness.

But in the course of meeting this guy and wanting to be alone together, and realizing that even if he left, it was going to be Friday night and we were close to a road, we thought, *It's a beautiful Friday night in early May, some kids are going to get the idea to come to this shelter, or some kind of group. So why don't we just pack everything up and move it all?* Even though we hadn't thought we would. Then we would camp somewhere along the trail, and Saturday morning we would finish whatever part of the trail we hadn't done and come back out.

We hadn't figured out yet exactly how we were going to do it. It didn't seem like too much, because it wasn't far and the hiking wasn't hard, although we didn't know where we were going to camp that night. At first we thought maybe we'd camp up on the ridge and have the view and walk down for water, but it turned out to be much too rocky to put a tent up there.

We took our time packing up and weren't even aware of this guy until I noticed that his towel was still there, laying on the lean-to. It was either his towel or his backpack. But basically, we were unconscious of him; he was off by himself. We went down to the stream and washed the dishes and walked a little ways and buried the leftover food and came back and took down the tent and packed both of our packs. There was no haste in any of it.

Finally, we were all ready to go. We had put on our packs

and passed by him as we were leaving. He was sitting in the lean-to, just sitting up. I don't think he was doing anything. I didn't see if he had a hard-on or anything like that. He was wearing those grey sweatpants. They were the only clothes I remember seeing him in.

And we left. "See you later," Rebecca said. "See you later," he said. "See you later," I said. There might have been one extra "See-you-later," and that was it. And I left—we left—intending to never see him again, assuming that that was absolutely it, bye-bye and no big deal. Just some guy and some campsite. We started up onto the Appalachian Trail.

About thirty minutes later, we got to a place that might have been the right place to turn. It was a little hard to estimate where we were. We stopped and took out the map. I remember kissing Rebecca and having a conversation with her. She was a little bit needy. I remember asking her if she wasn't getting enough kisses. She seemed like...there was a little bit of an issue going on but she couldn't really say. It wasn't a big deal, but she was just a bit wanting.

Now, as I think about it, I don't think the whole thing was an aspect of closure. I do feel like the conversations we had, and the references...maybe they were closure. I don't know. It's one of the things I talk about a lot with Kris: if Rebecca knew she was leaving. I know her spirit still exists, but her body is gone, the physical relationship that we had. I almost feel like she knew it, not knew it, but knew it.

In any case, we were kissing and looking at the map. We had figured out which way to turn and were discussing how we wanted to go around this loop. It's a loop trail, so we decided to go that way, and when we got to the fork we would go east. We didn't decide then where we were going to camp.

Just as I was putting the map back in the top pocket of Rebecca's backpack—she had a really nice internal frame backpack—I heard a sneering voice saying, "You're lost *already?*"

We turned around, and there he was, about thirty feet away. We were startled, but not a lot. It was strange: *Huh, what are you doing here? You were just hanging at the campsite.* It was too fast. We had only taken a couple of extra minutes to look at the map and he was there, so there was an uncanny feeling. Why was he walking in the same direction as us?

His hands...were draped very casually over a rifle, which was behind his head, across his shoulders. I think he was wearing a knapsack too. It looked like holding the gun that way was part of how he was used to walking. When I think about it now, it reminds me of how soldiers in Israel are when they have carried a gun for so many years and it's like an extension of themselves. They're completely comfortable. That's what he was like with this gun.

So he said, "Are you lost already?" and I said, "No, are you?" What I thought was, *Get the fuck out of my life. Leave me alone. I don't need you, I don't want you, I don't want to talk to you, I don't want to see you anymore, what the fuck is that gun doing across your shoulders?*

But all I said was, "No, are you?" and we started walking. By the time he got to the place where we had been, we were already far away. He never joined us, it never became a conversation between the three of us. He kept walking straight, or we thought he kept walking straight.

We turned around to look back a lot as we walked. We wondered what he was doing with a gun. There was no hunting season at that time. What was he shooting?

I said, "Maybe he's just going to a two or three o'clock shift at some factory." I thought he had a truck parked somewhere. It wouldn't have made sense...well, it might have made sense that he would have walked all the way up to the shelter. He had said he arrived at the site at 2:00 in the morning. I don't know, somehow I thought he was going back to wherever his truck was, he was going to go to work. There's a parking symbol here on the map. If he had really been going to work, he might have left a car there and was going to pick it up. That was what I hoped.

We looked back a lot. I looked back a lot. But I didn't feel like we were being followed. We never, in a million years...you just don't...I don't feel badly...I mean, I do feel badly, but it never occurred to me that someone would do something that creepy. People don't just follow you and shoot you. It doesn't make any sense.

So we got going, and it was a pretty hard trail, a lot of uphill. We got up to the ridge on the eastern side of the loop, and there was a pretty view. The ridge dropped off steeply, and we could look at the hills on the other side. There was water down in the valley, too, but we couldn't see it.

Walking the ridge took most of the afternoon. We got to the top of the ridge at about noon, where the main trail and a side trail intersected. There wasn't a good place to camp. We would have had to walk a long way down for water. So we just kept walking. Parts of the trail were like rock climbing, and I got really tired.

By mistake, we walked all the way up to this peak with our packs on. It was really hard, but we had a beautiful view of the lake. Then we came down and got a bit lost a few minutes further on the trail, until we finally turned the corner. It was all taking longer than I thought it would, and I was getting tired, but it wasn't late at all.

I remember one incident that really endeared Rebecca to me. I was lightheaded, that lightheadedness that comes from being tired. There was going to be a place in a little while where we'd planned to rest, but I really wanted to stop then. I felt like I wasn't being tough enough, but I told Rebecca anyway. And we stopped. Right there. Exactly there. It was fine. We ate something and kissed a little and had fun.

We were still talking about the guy and looking back a lot.

I'm almost positive now that he wasn't following us the whole day. I think he figured out where we were going, turned around after we were out of sight, and took the western part of the loop to the campsite. It feels like he waited for us, rather than following us the whole trail. I know he could have, but it doesn't feel like it.

As the trail brought us near the stream, we started looking for a place to camp. First we found a place in the middle of the trail where someone had built some circles for a campsite, which made Rebecca think maybe there wasn't very much flat land. We put our packs down and bushwhacked toward the stream to see what it looked like, but it was very overgrown. So we went back and started strolling, looking around for a place to set up our tent.

And I saw this opening. It led to a campsite right off the trail and it was nice. Then we followed a little less of a trail which led to the stream, and we were in a lovely campsite, a dream come true sort of place. It's creepy when you think about it, how he was watching the whole time, knowing about that campsite on the trail, predicting where we'd go. He knew where we were exactly.

The campsite was like a gift, exactly what we wanted. I remember saying, "We're off the trail, there's no way he can find us." You see, he was still an issue, but it was the kind of issue that you have in the back of your mind until you get out of the woods. But an issue, nevertheless. Like, *Good, we're not at the campsite close to the trail.* (Sigh.)

But it was hot and there was a gurgling stream and the sky was blue and I loved her. We were having a running conversation all day about moss. Doesn't it sound like we were having fun together?

J: Yeah.

C: We had running conversations about different things. We had one about gliding, too.

She had asked about what was going on in Ithaca. I hadn't told her yet because it was full of feelings and I just hadn't gotten in the mood. I hadn't forgotten that she wanted to know, though. Sometimes she would talk a lot, I mean, a lot a lot, and I would listen, and then she would remember that I hadn't been talking, she would get me to talk and then I would talk a lot. Some things I would wait to be asked about. She got good—she would remember to ask.

I was walking first when we left Birch Run, and I remember asking if I was walking fast enough, because I always felt a bit greener than her. We switched later and she was walking first.

J: Could you walk side by side?

C: No, not much. Right when we left, that place where he saw us, was wide enough. In fact, I think we were holding hands for a little bit, but that wasn't very long and then it was single file.

(Sigh.) So this running conversation was about whether there was ever a patch of moss big enough to lay down on. And there it was. Not exactly moss, but some kind of plant that was so green and so soft, you can't imagine. I was so excited as soon as I saw it.

It's really creepy that he must have set himself up to be able to see us. As we moved around the campsite he had to have repositioned himself to keep watching.

We didn't set up the tent right away because it was still light, 3:30, maybe 4:00 in the afternoon. It wasn't going to get dark for hours and there was nothing we needed to do except hang out, rest, eat dinner and eventually set up the tent and go to sleep.

We decided we would make iced tea, but we had to boil water first. Rebecca had a sore throat, so we made high vitamin-C iced tea. She boiled water on the stove and I opened up my pack which had most of the food in it. I was snacking a little bit, and

Firebrand Books

141 The Commons

Ithaca, New York 14850

Firebrand Books

Firebrand Books is an award-winning feminist and lesbian publishing house committed to producing quality work in a wide variety of genres by ethnically and racially diverse authors.

Firebrand titles are available through bookstores nationally and directly by mail from us. If you would like to receive a free catalog, please return this card or call (607) 272-0000.

Name _____

Address _____

City _____ State _____ Zip _____

she was too. We weren't really hungry because we had had lunch. She poured the hot tea into the canteen and I stuck it in a little rocky place in the stream so it wouldn't float away. It got really cold and we drank it.

We had a funny conversation about it tasting like sweet juice. It was Satya's canteen and I figured out that she must have left Kool-Aid in it once. When I checked it out later with Satya, she said that years ago she used to make bug juice on camping trips, and probably there was some residue left, which we could still taste.

Then we laid out the tent and the fly by the stream. It was wet on the moss, but not through the tent fly because it's waterproof. Just a little cool. God it was nice. Stream, sunshine, breeze, trees above. I brought over some chocolate. We were sexual a bit. Playful, rolling around. The bugs were biting, so we rolled up inside the tent fly so they wouldn't bother us.

In all the reports it always says that we were making love when the shooting happened. We weren't really in the middle of heavy sex. We were playing—kissing and rolling around.

At some point I think Rebecca had said take off your shorts, and we were having—not having oral sex with a capital O.S., but...we were...playing. It was all really nice, kind of idyllic. In fact, very idyllic...

Why I mention that is that I was only partially dressed when the shooting happened. Rebecca was fully dressed. The image in the reports is that we were in the middle of a passionate sex act. I have always said "making love" because I am paranoid they will discredit our relationship by saying, "Oh, they were only playing around."

Hanging out with Rebecca, chatting, playing, having fun. We rolled off the side of the tarp and played games with each other, laid in the sun...

I remember saying to Rebecca, "Do you want to set up the tent and get serious about this?" And she said, "No, let's stay out here."

I think that's the last normal exchange of conversation we had. I was lying down, on my side, and she was lower than me, but near me, on this side, and one second it was like that, and the next second there was an explosion, an incredible explosion, and my arm exploded.

The world just, the world exploded, the world just exploded. How can the world explode?

The world doesn't explode, you know?

I knew something had happened to my arm and something had happened to the earth. My mind said, *Earthquake? Volcano?* Those were my first thoughts. Then I thought, *Volcanos don't make you bleed.*

The tarp that we were on was green, then all of a sudden there was red, splattered everywhere. My mind couldn't absorb the information fast enough to understand what had happened. Rebecca said, "Where did you get shot, Claudia?" She somehow knew.

I don't know how, but she knew. I had no idea what had happened. I saw the red of my blood on the tarp, and I knew something had happened to my arm, or to the earth, or...but my first thought was that the world had exploded. Rebecca knew. And I never had time to ask her how she knew. I think I got hit three times in those next twenty-five or thirty seconds.

I don't remember exactly when but we said to each other, "He came back." I sat up, I remember seeing the blood, and...there were more shots. I started screaming. Screaming. SCREAMING! I remember screaming, "Stop!" and then, "Enough!"

That was when I got shot in the neck and possibly the cheek. Rebecca said, "Get down!" She hadn't gotten hit because I was in his line of fire. Rebecca was laying behind me so somehow my body was shielding her.

She said, "Get down," and I got down. She was the person

who was thinking. A bullet hit me again in the head. That was when Rebecca said, "Run behind the tree."

I went first. I ran for the tree, and almost all in one motion, I was behind it. She ran second. That's when she got hit. Twice. After I moved she got hit. Ahhh.

Then there was one more shot.

We were behind the tree and I was running my mouth. How are we going to get out of here, how are we going to get out of herehowarewegoingtogetoutofherehowwegetoutofhere, what are we going to do...Speed! What are we going to do, what're we going to do, what are we going to do. Over by the tarp, I had said to Rebecca, "I might die, I really might die." Now, behind the tree, I said to myself, *I'm not going to die.* It was inconceivable that I would die.

She wasn't saying much, she wasn't saying anything, I don't remember. Then she said, "What are we going to do?"

J: Were you holding each other?

C: Un-uh. We were near each other. I was still running my mouth. I would have run my mouth for two hours before I had thought to do anything different. Then Rebecca said to me, "Stop the bleeding." She was so smart. "Stop the bleeding." Of course. That's what you do with any wound.

Get down. Get behind the tree. Stop the bleeding. Those commands saved my life. A series of lights went off in my mind and I got it: Stop the bleeding. This is an emergency. At that moment, I switched. It was a crucial point for me, because that was the first time I came back from my frantic paralysis, and changed to hyper-alert mode. Every resource in my being became engaged in that moment in saving myself. And in saving Rebecca.

"Stop the bleeding" was the last statement she made with any lucidity. In that moment, she both saved my life and also let go of the responsibility for our safety. And I took it. It felt like her spirit left her; she knew she was dying. She was leaning up against the tree, wasn't moving much. At one point I felt like she wanted me to lay in her arms and die, like Romeo and Juliet. I know she didn't want me to die, but if we were going to—and that was one of the possibilities, that we were both going to die right there—that we should do it together.

The whole thing became a kind of time warp: three hundred hours condensed into ten minutes. Once, I said, "What about Anne and Satya?" And Rebecca said, "What about Evelyn?"

I don't know how long we were behind the tree, but apparently it was long enough for him. He fled.

J: You didn't know that though.

C: I didn't fucking know that. I didn't have any idea what to do except I knew we needed help so badly that I couldn't believe it. I knew that I had to get help, just had to.

I don't know why or when or what gave me the fucking guts, but I went out from behind the tree. The only reason why he didn't shoot me then was that he wasn't there. He had twenty-five more rounds of ammunition.

J: Where was the most bleeding?

C: On me? My neck. So I got up and went. I got some clothing and a towel. I pressed a red shirt to the back of Rebecca's neck and I got a white towel for me. It was just the right size to hold really tightly around my neck, which slowed the flow of blood.

Before I had the towel around my neck, I was much more vulnerable. About then I realized, *I'm going to live.* I thought, *It must have been a BB gun. He must have been shooting a BB gun. I'm going to live.* And when I realized I could live, I think I expected that she would live too. I'm sure I did. Somehow it didn't occur to me that her bullets were in different places. It just occurred to me that if I could live, then she could live.

I was still running my mouth. I think I spoke continuously from the time of the shots until I left—some kind of panic.

I was starting to talk about us walking out of there to get

help. I had already gone to get the towel and the shirts, so I was not afraid to walk around anymore. I went to the packs and got out sweatpants for me, and both pairs of our sneakers. I put my sneakers on...and set her sneakers down beside her. She was feeling around for the sneakers with her hands. She couldn't see...she couldn't see. She was starting to go blind. Neither one of us totally understood that she was starting to go blind. Then I handed her her sneakers but she couldn't put them on. So I put them on for her. I still thought that we were both going. Later on the police didn't understand why the sneakers were tied so tight.

By then, everything had kicked in in my body to protect me from the pain, and I practically didn't even know anymore that I had been shot. I knew it, but I wasn't feeling it.

And I started saying, "Rebecca, c'mon get up, we gotta go, we gotta go, gotta go," and talking to her and talking to her and she wasn't saying anything. Whatever decisions her spirit was making, she was becoming less and less present, less and less of her was around. Talking became harder for her. She couldn't answer me and she was in great pain.

I still thought we were both going to be okay. I would help her; we would just walk. I tried to pick her up four or five times, and every time I collapsed. She was heavy. I started to panic...just running my mouth. "Rebecca, Rebecca, don't let him get you. We've got to get out of here."

She tried to get up once by herself and made it a little bit away from the big tree. There were two small trees close by, maybe four inches in diameter, about eighteen inches away from each other. I helped her get up, and I said, "Hold onto the trees. The trees have always been your friends." She tried. She really tried, but she couldn't stand. She wheezed and then collapsed. After that I realized that I couldn't possibly carry her. I had thought she could walk leaning on me. I had no idea how far it was. Finally I had to accept the fact that she couldn't walk on her own at all. This was maybe...I couldn't say exactly. It could be four minutes from the shooting, it could be five, it could be eight, that's all. No time has passed at all.

After she collapsed one last time, she said, "It really hurts a lot," and I said, "Where?" And she said, "In my back." I turned her over and I saw where the bullet had entered her back through two layers of clothing. I asked her if I should try and cut the bullet out. I thought of that, what you see on television. Thank god I didn't: It would have been so awful because the bullet ended up right under her breastbone. I know that now, but I didn't know it then. But she said no. I was scared she would bleed to death from my cutting. What they told me recently is that had she been on an operating table when she took that shot in her liver, she still would have died. It was fatal. She wouldn't have died from the other wound in her head. That was similar to the wounds I had. Her skull was fractured but she probably wouldn't have had brain damage.

I helped her lie down, and when I looked at her, I thought her eyes had rolled back in her head. I don't really know, though, because later on when the police showed me the photographs, her irises were there and brown. I think I saw her last with no eyes. It was hard. Her lips didn't have any color in them; they blended with her skin. I thought I felt a tiny bit of a pulse and tried to give her mouth to mouth resuscitation. I didn't know it very well and it didn't seem to help anyway.

I had to choose. Earlier, I had said, "I have go for help," and she didn't want me to leave. I had to say, "I've got to go, I've got to go, I have to go." I was terrified.

It was hard to realize that I had to leave her, that I had to go for help. It was the hardest thing I ever did in my life. Especially this: *We* were going to get out of there, and all of a sudden, *I* had to go.

I explained to her that I had to go and get help. I got up, and she was really worried about money. I had said I needed money, it was my first response in that panic, that I needed my wallet. One of the last things she said to me was about money. She said, "Your wallet is in my shirt." She had gotten money to go out to dinner in D.C., which was also in her shirt, and she remembered that I had put my wallet in there.

So I took the wallet out of her pocket. Then I realized I needed the map, so I went to look for the map. I remembered that Rebecca had had the map last, and remembered seeing her set it down somewhere, on a very definite place. So I looked around, and I couldn't find it. I went back to her. I thought, *I have to have the map,* so I went back and I looked, and it was right there where she had set it, still sitting on the stone of the firepit with a rock on top of it. I grabbed it. Then I went back to her and I was talking with...still talking to her. I have the money and I have the map. I knew it was going to get dark, I didn't know how soon, so I thought, *I have to have a flashlight.* Anne had lent me a flashlight, a powerful little maglite. I knew it was in my pack, so I went to my pack, and looked, and couldn't find it. I went back to Rebecca, and then I said to myself, *No, you have to have the flashlight,* because I was getting ready to leave. I went back and it was right there, in my pack, and I took it. I had to do everything twice.

I had my wallet and my flashlight and my map and I was looking at her, telling her that I was just about to leave, and I was, and then I thought, *I'm cold. Maybe she's cold.* So I put everything down, ran back to our packs and took out both our sleeping bags, and covered her up with them. She had a really warm, wonderful, heavy down bag. Later, I worried because her back was on the ground. I was also very worried about her breathing, but I thought that I had heard that a person's breathing slows way down if they're in a coma.

I remembered that I was cold, too, and I realized it was going to get colder when the sun set, so I put on a sweatshirt. My T-shirt was drenched with blood. I meant to take my sleeping bag, also, which was very small. I thought if it got really cold I could wrap it around me, but moments later, I forgot it.

I took my little package—I had these three things and no place to put them because I was wearing sweatpants and a sweatshirt but I was scared to put them in the pockets because they were side pockets and I was afraid something would fall out and I would lose it. So I just clenched them, the entire walk. Except when I had to stop and look at the map. Oh, god it was scary. And then I told her I was going. No, that was before, when I was getting ready. By the time I left, she couldn't talk to me, she couldn't talk anymore.

I didn't think about it at the time, but I didn't get to say good-bye. I was pretty panicked. I feel badly about that. I know it's okay, and she knows that I said good-bye, but I feel guilty. The truth is, it wasn't a romantic parting. It was an escape. I was almost dying, and trying to get her help...and I left. I walked up the trail from where we were by the stream. Right before I got to the main trail, I felt myself pulled back. I thought, *I want to go back.* I couldn't think of any reason to, but I was physically pulled. It was hard—I couldn't have gone back, I never would have left again. That's the feeling I have. I would have died. I wouldn't have gone for help. I couldn't have beared leaving her again.

My spirit might have been pulling me back and hers might have said, *Go. Go, I love you. Go!* I was bleeding. Something in me said, *Walk.* I turned left onto the main trail. I didn't know who was there. He could have been. I was terrified. I know now that he wasn't there but I didn't know then. Can you believe I did this?

All of a sudden, smack in the center of the path, there was this Coke can. Classic. I knew, just knew. It smacked of *I hate you, I hate nature.* Right in the middle of the path. There hadn't been any trash on the trail before. The police saw two cigarette butts the whole way. There was this Coke Classic can right in the center of the trail, saying, *I hate people who care about nature.* Who knows if it had any connection, I was just scared. The path wasn't a hiking trail anymore, more like a four-wheel drive access road, pretty smooth, with grass growing over it. But it was uphill. I remember thinking, *Oh no, uphill.* I wanted to run, but I knew I couldn't, that I had to walk. *Just walk, you don't need to run. Just walk, and keep walking.* I was having trouble breathing, with all the blood in my mouth. I didn't know whether to swallow or spit out. It hurt a lot to swallow and my ear started to hurt, too. My arm was burning—the whole time I was walking there was a fire burning inside my arm. The wound on my neck gurgled, like air was coming through the wrong places. I was spitting out a lot of blood and...things. So I just walked—and walked and walked and walked uphill and just walked. Twice, there were big logs which had fallen over the trail. That depressed me because it made me think they couldn't take a four wheel drive vehicle in. It turns out that they did, and they cut the logs with a chain saw. I didn't know they would do that. I thought we'd be walking back, I thought *I'd* be walking back to help find her.

Five or ten minutes after I left, I saw a little bird, on the left side of the path, sitting in the sunshine. It was black and white, in a distinct pattern. It sounds a little corny, but when I saw the bird, I knew. I didn't fully know, but I knew. I even thought the black and white bird made sense because Rebecca was part white, part Puerto Rican.

A little while later, I noticed that the forest was full of bird sounds. I was angry that the forest sounds were the same, that they were sweet. Were they talking about Rebecca? There had been shots. I could still hear them. Were the birds talking about the horrible noises?

It seemed to take a long time to get to the intersection where we had taken the left part of the loop. When I got there, I was terrified that I would meet him. I felt scared all the time, but I thought about it only some of the time. At that juncture, I thought about it.

I passed the place where we had met him on the trail. I knew I should head for a road, not a trail or her car, a road. I kept checking the map, at every intersection, finding where I was. I was particularly scared he was going to be at the parking area I was going to pass by. Maybe he had a car there? I was scared all the time, but...sometimes I was more scared.

J: How did you know it was him?

C: Because we had seen him with the gun earlier in the afternoon and he was the only other person we had seen. There wasn't any other human being who would know where we were. No one else on the whole planet could have done it. We had seen him, and no one else, with a gun over his shoulders. There was never any doubt that it was him.

I thought I would see him at every bend in the trail. I became slightly more confident as I walked that that wasn't going to happen. That wasn't very confident, though—from terrified to terrified. I got to Ridge Road and had to choose whether to go left or right. Shippensburg Road, the biggest, most populated road in the area, was north, so I made a right onto Ridge.

It was a very quiet state forest road, fairly wide and covered with light brownish gravel. I was glad for the lightness of the stones, because it made the whole world seem lighter. As it got dark, a black road would have made it seem darker.

I was coughing a lot and having trouble swallowing. Sometimes I spit the fluid in my mouth out. My arm still burned. There were no cars. I was amazed, I was walking in the middle of a road and there simply were no cars and no houses. I thought about Rebecca, and also about what I would say when I saw a car. I would say, "You must help me. I've been shot." I would leave no room for anyone to not help me.

I remember I was thinking that if I saw a house, whether or not I should break in. Would that just make it worse? Will he be there? I always considered the possibility that he would be there.

As I was walking, I realized that there was a shorter way to get to Shippensburg Road, but it meant going back into the woods on a half road, half trail. By then it was starting to get dark and I said, "No trails. No woods. Just road." I realize now that since he was running, he probably would try to stay away from roads. So my guiding spirit, whatever it was, was telling me to go completely differently than him, which was: You go on the road where people might come. He, on the other had, was choosing—and I didn't know this then—off the road, off the trail, because he didn't want to be seen. I wanted to be seen, and staying on the road was a really good decision.

Once, I thought I saw some movement in the woods on the left side of the road. I freaked. I couldn't turn my head to the left at all, nor all the way around the other way, because my neck was in excruciating pain. So the only way for me to look around was to turn my whole body in a circle. So once in a while, I turned completely around. As I say this now, it sounds like it must be someone else. But how else could I know all this? I must have done it.

So I stared at that spot in the darkening woods out of the corner of my eye, and I put my hands up over my head and shouted, "If you are a human being, don't shoot me, please don't shoot me." I had my hands up in the air for about a hundred feet, saying, "If you're human, don't shoot me, please don't kill me, you've already killed one person, please don't shoot me. Please, don't kill me—" That was not, *I surrender*, but...*And if you're gonna do it, fucking shoot me, in the fucking face, shoot me in my heart.* Nothing happened.

I hadn't spoken the whole way until that point; I had no one to speak to. I just was talking in my own mind. But then I shouted out loud, and every time I did, there was that painful gurgling in my throat, the air getting into my neck in the wrong places. I didn't know that was why, though. All I knew was that I was bleeding there. I gave no thought to any of my wounds except for the one in my arm.

Something helped me to keep climbing past the steady, uphill grades in the road. I would remember seeing them a few minutes before, but not walking over them. I couldn't believe how far it was.

It was dusk. I had been walking for over three hours. In front of me, suddenly—headlights and a car coming down my road. The towel around my neck, which used to be white, was blood red. I took it off and waved it. The next thing I remember...is standing at the side of the road and watching the car go by. It didn't stop. It was a brand new-looking Blazer, brown. There might have even been lights on the side of the car—maybe an emergency vehicle? I didn't imagine it, this happened...and they didn't stop. It wasn't him. A man might have been driving, young, and two women. I could see the face of the woman in the passenger's seat, and it didn't stop. I was shocked.

So I kept on walking. I knew I must be getting somewhere even though the road seemed infinitely long. Time was important, but when I decided that I was not going to take the shortcut, I was also deciding that it was okay to take longer, even though I wanted to get help to Rebecca right away. I guess I knew it was more important to arrive someplace safely than it was to hurry, because there was no way I could hurry and live. I wanted to run but I knew I couldn't. I'm glad I didn't go into the woods. Right now, the idea of going into the woods is incredibly terrifying. It's really sad because I loved the woods.

I began to hear the sounds of cars up ahead. At the same time, I saw a house on my left. I considered breaking in. There might be people. Or it could be empty, a summer house with no phone hooked up. Then I thought, he could be there. What if I got trapped? It's just going to make more trouble if I break in. It's not going to make it faster.

I passed the house and around the next bend was the main road. I looked in both directions, and at my map, and decided not to walk any more. I would wait for a car.

It was dark by then, so I turned on my flashlight. Almost immediately, I saw headlights coming toward me. I stepped right into the middle of the lane, making huge, slow circles of light with my flashlight. My arm had arced around my body six or seven times before they got close enough to stop. Even when I sensed the car slowing down, I still didn't move out of the lane, and I kept making more circles.

It wasn't him. It was an old eight-cylinder car with two teenage boys inside, sixteen or seventeen, local kids. I went to the driver's side and when the one there unrolled his window, I said exactly what I had planned to say: "You must help me. I've been shot."

He started to turn the car around and I panicked, "Where are you going, where are you going?" He said, "We're just turning the car around."

He finished and the kid on the passenger's side got out and opened his door and the door in back. I started to get in back, and he said, "No, you get in front." He was really nice. I did, and closed the door, and he got in the back, and we went, fast.

"My name is Claudia Brenner," I said slowly. "We were camping on the Rocky Knob Trail which is off the Appalachian Trail. There is someone else there. She was also shot. Her name is Rebecca Wight.

I told them this over and over, and they repeated it back. My name, the name of the trail. Off the Appalachian. And her name is Rebecca Wight. They told me they'd get me to help. They did incredibly well. Some unknown, bloody, unbelievable human being had flagged down their car, and they took me and the information in: This is what happened, you were shot, this is where she is. I didn't ask who they were.

"Where are we going to go?"

"Shippensburg."

"How far is it?"

"Fifteen minutes."

"Fifteen minutes!"

"Yeah."

We were driving fast, and I said, "Please don't wreck, please don't wreck." He was careful. "My name is Claudia Brenner. We were camping on the Rocky Knob Trail..."

I realized, for the first time, that we were going to get help. I began to feel a trace of the pain because there was a little bit of room for it.

"What's in Shippensburg?"

"A police and fire station."

They weren't talking very much, scared probably, and shy. They were shy country boys. Eventually I said, "Talk to me, just talk to me about anything." I couldn't just sit, the minutes were so long. One said, "I could turn on the radio?" He did. I can't remember what song was playing.

I still couldn't swallow and kept spitting out into my towel. The kid who was driving—I think his name was Cory. I later found out that one was named Cory and the other was Chris. Cory had a white plastic cup, and he said to me, "Um, that's my spitting cup. I just started chewing a couple of minutes ago, there's not much in it. If you want to spit in it you can use it." It was such an incredibly sweet offer, for a seventeen-year-old kid to let me spit in his spitting cup. He offered twice: "There's not much in it, I haven't been using it very long." I don't remember if I said no thanks or what.

About five minutes into the trip I asked what time it was. It was quite dark by then. Cory asked Chris, "What time is it, Chris?" Chris looked at his watch and said, "8:57."

I was still clutching my map and my wallet and my flashlight. They saved me. There was no way I would have made it without a flashlight. How would I have flagged anyone down? I would have had to scream. You can't stand in the road—maybe I would have. It would have been scary, though. But with a light I felt like I had a communicator, a signal. And I had to look twice for it. I couldn't have walked to Shippensburg. Fifteen minutes is ten or fifteen miles.

J: Were you crying?

C: I was functioning. I didn't get to cry until much later. I don't remember when I started—days later.

Finally, they told me that we were on the outskirts of Shippensburg. I said, "Where is it, where is it?" The police and fire station was one small, quiet building. I opened the car door and got out. The night was warm, and a uniformed man with a beard was sitting outside on a folding chair in the driveway of the station. I don't know if he was a police officer or fireman or what.

"I've been shot," I said to him.

He got up and said to the two boys, "You stay here." He put his arm around me—he was really nice—and brought me inside. Several more officers were inside, and immediately, there were people on the phone—(snap) instantly.

The entire police department was a counter and two large wooden desks where the local police routinely answered calls from neighbors with dog complaints and issued parking tickets and summonses. One of them said, "Sit down," and I sat in a swivel chair behind one of the wooden desks.

"What happened?"

"I've been shot and Rebecca is still in the woods. There's a woman in the woods and she's hurt real badly."

"What's your name?"

I took my driver's license out from my wallet and gave it to them.

"She's been hurt," I said. I didn't want them to deal with me now. "We have to go find her, we have to go get her."

"You're not going anywhere. You're going to get help."

I said, "No, we have to find her," and took out the map. I don't know what I must have looked like. Bloody. I had blood all over. As I went from police station to hospital to hospital that night, I got more and more of the blood washed off. I couldn't get all of the blood out of my hair until days later. Even after a week, there was still blood under my fingernails.

I heard someone on the phone saying numbers. Maybe they were checking my ID, or maybe they were just calling for the ambulance. I explained where she was, and they kept saying, "You were on the Appalachian Trail?" And I kept correcting them, "We were on the Rocky Knob Trail which is off the Appalachian Trail."

Speaking was hard. My throat would gurgle painfully every time. I still couldn't swallow and my ear hurt too. I would take...well, I would try to take a deep breath, decide to swallow, cringe, swallow, and explain again that it was the Rocky Knob Trail.

I made a circle on my map where I thought we had been. In the end, they gave me a map showing exactly where we were, and I was off just by a little bit. In fact, I made a big enough circle so that they found her just about at the center of it. They organized a search party immediately. By the time I left there were people by the police station, outside. People from the town had run to the station when they heard.

J: To help?

C: Either to help or just to see. I said to the officers, "I want to make some phone calls." I reached for the phone, intending to call Evelyn? Anne? I'm not sure who I intended to call but I knew that I needed to notify our people.

They said, "No phone calls now. You have to get medical attention." I remember feeling frustrated because I wanted to call Anne and tell her what had happened. I wanted Rebecca's sister Evelyn to come up fast because we needed help.

I vividly remember my flashlight laying on the officer's

desk, with some blood on the side. I forgot to take it with me later, and it got lost.

The police were trying to figure out what county we had been in. Now I understand that they had to do that in order to get the right state police notified, but at the time I didn't understand why they were wasting time with the county. *Why aren't you looking for her now?*

I had to give up the map to the search party so that they could go find her. I had to trust them, trust that they were going to look for her. After they all went out, the guy with the beard came running back in and said, "Her name is Rebecca?" I got it, that they were going to call out to her in the woods. I nodded and he ran back out. He wanted to make sure they were going to call her by the right name, Becky or whatever she was called. That was the feeling I had, that they wanted to call her by her name so they wouldn't scare her. I can see them in the woods now, yelling, "Rebecca!" I'm sure her spirit heard.

Soon, the ambulance was there with the stretcher. They wanted me to lay down on it and all I wanted to do was go and look for Rebecca. My neck had started to hurt badly on the car ride to Shippensburg, but even then I still thought I would just be stitched up and return to the campsite. Now, for the first time, I considered the possibility that I wasn't going to get to go back and look for her.

There was a low wall, like a counter that you would do business over. I started to walk out to the ambulance but they insisted that I lay down on the stretcher. I lay down and was strapped in, and then they realized that there was no way to get the stretcher through the opening in the counter. So I had to get up out of the stretcher, walk through the opening and then lay down on the stretcher again.

A medic examined me through all the blood. I heard someone talking about stopping traffic at the light. Then I was in the ambulance, flat on my back. Some people put on gloves because of AIDS and all the blood. An E.M.T. who rode in the back with me administering an IV ignored the blood from my body that was getting all over him. Too concerned to stop and put on gloves, or too far removed from AIDS to think about it. I didn't talk to anybody about Rebecca once I was in the ambulance because they weren't the people that were going to be looking for her.

The police escorted the ambulance out of Shippensburg, heading for the hospital in Chambersburg. The ride hurt. You expect an ambulance to be comfortable, but the bumps made me aware of my wounds and I was coughing and I hated the oxygen.

They finally got me to the hospital in Chambersburg. In the Emergency Room, they took vital signs and x-rays and asked me what happened again. Everything took a long time. It was funny—I received urgent medical attention in between long periods of waiting.

After they took x-rays, the nurse asked me who I wanted to call. I gave her Anne's phone number, but the hospital wanted to call my parents.

"No, I want Anne to call my parents," I said. And they said, "We want your parent's phone number," and I said, "You can have my parent's phone number but I don't want you to call them." Not that I didn't want my parents to know, but I needed help and I wanted Anne first. In the end, the nurse never called anybody.

Then I gave them Evelyn's phone number. It turns out they didn't call her either. I understand now that they couldn't call her and say, "We have your sister's companion here. She was shot five times and we don't know where your sister is." I didn't understand that at the time, though, because in my mind Rebecca was still alive, so I wanted Evelyn to come fast so she would be there when they got Rebecca. I didn't know what had happened, and I was holding on to this tiny chance—

I had to trust that strangers would do a good job of finding Rebecca. Each segment of my journey took me farther from her. Chambersburg was another twenty miles from Shippensburg, which was already fifteen minutes from the place I had walked for hours to reach. No one in Chambersburg would know where the Rocky Knob Trail was on the Appalachian Trail.

The state police came while I was in Emergency. One officer in a blue jacket stood at the end of the bed and listened and heard me as I explained what had happened and where we were. Fallen logs. The Rocky Knob Trail off the Appalachian Trail. Take the loop in the direction of the creek. Look for a place where there is a fire ring close to the trail and near it there will be a path leading toward the stream. The campsite is down the path, and Rebecca will be under a blue sleeping bag. He took notes and repeated back what I said, and I finally believed that they would take care of finding Rebecca. After that, I knew I had to let go of the search. It was up to the state police to find her.

I finally let some of my attention to be focused on my own injuries. The Chambersburg hospital had called an ear, nose, and throat specialist. The doctor cut my shirt off, examined my head, neck, and chest briefly, and then I never saw him again. The next thing I knew, the nurse informed me I needed to go to Hershey Medical Center in a helicopter.

I had no interest in going on a helicopter ride at all. I didn't understand why they couldn't help me already. At *this* hospital. Wasn't it good enough? Couldn't they stitch me up? I heard the words "trauma center." I had barely accepted the idea that I needed some medical attention, but a trauma center? I thought the doctor was overreacting. What was so special about Hershey? I didn't consider myself "in shock" or "experiencing a trauma." I was annoyed that they weren't getting me patched up so that I could go back to help locate Rebecca.

I remember they made me stay cold. My saying I was cold

meant I wasn't in shock.

The nurse asked, "Have you ever flown on a helicopter before?" as though I was a preschooler. Someone told me that in twenty-eight minutes the 'copter would be there, and then I was left alone to wait. Twenty-eight minutes sounded like forever. But there was no choice. I was stuck there on a table, aware of every detail of every moment, flat on my back.

There was one person, maybe a medical technician, who kept checking in on me whenever she could. It wasn't her job to be there. She would hold my hand and tell me how long it had been so far, and what was going to happen. I never found out her name. She said, "I'll walk you to the helicopter—well, we're wheeling you, but..." I was extremely grateful for that human contact during the long minutes it took for the helicopter to arrive.

When the helicopter finally came, I heard them talking about transport regulations. They had to strap me onto a straight board, which hurt. I kept saying, "Be careful of my neck." For several days, people had to lift my neck and shoulders when they moved me. Between laying flat on my back and having velcro splints stiffening my legs, I had a hard time keeping up my constant surveillance of everything going on around me.

The helicopter staff were well trained, though. One woman took the time to tell me what it would feel like to lift off, and that it would be noisy. She noticed my extreme pain in swallowing and produced a simple but miraculous device which I used for many days after: a suction tube which took the saliva out of my mouth.

She didn't ask event-related questions, and I was grateful for her professionalism. I was choosing, very consciously, to be quiet. There was no information to be had about Rebecca from those people. Days later, the woman stopped in to see me. It was part of their service to follow up.

I still didn't understand what the problem was, I didn't

know why they had to take to me to Hershey, I didn't think I needed a trauma unit. I didn't even know what a trauma unit was. I wanted to go back and look for Rebecca. I wanted Rebecca to be okay.

' ONE '

Rebecca and I met at a Women's Week committee meeting. The fall of 1985 was my first semester in a three-year graduate program in architecture at Virginia Tech, and within a few months of being there I knew I needed to meet like-minded women. I thought surely the weekly gathering of students, faculty, staff, and members of the wider Blacksburg community interested in planning the annual seven days of women's events in the spring would turn up some lesbians and feminists.

I had just moved to a new city and was starting a new career. I had left Ithaca, New York, where my lover of almost nine years, Anne, and I were at the tail end of what most people would call a laborious break-up. We had met in 1977. I had been socializing in the "Lavender Hill" circle: "cool faggots and dykes" from New York City who had bought country land in West Danby, outside of Ithaca. It was the artsy crowd. I was twenty-one and had just graduated from Cornell. Anne was a new friend to that crowd of people, thirty-two, wise but very funky, a straight woman on the road to becoming a lesbian.

Anne had been moving toward wanting to be with women for several years. Clear blue eyes, fine light-brown hair, lean—she was raising her blonde five-year-old daughter, Satya. After many "chance" meetings at the Blue Angel (the downtown gay dive), some conspicuous flirting, and one outdoor arts festival, we became lovers.

By 1985 when I moved to Blacksburg, the lover part of our relationship was history. We had tried various permutations of nonmonogamy, but all were torture for me. Over the difficult, extended period before I moved, even as it became more and more clear that we were romantically incompatible, Anne insisted that she wanted to remain partners with me. "Breakup" was a foreign concept to her, while for me the idea of a "life partner," given our circumstances, seemed too unconventional. Could we remain a family if we were each involved with other lovers?

What was true, however, was that Anne and Satya were undeniably my family. Even though our ties as partners waxed and waned, and my moving to Virginia put an additional strain on the relationship, I still considered Ithaca my home and planned to continue using Anne's house as a base. We were, in what would later become common queer vocabulary, "chosen family."

It's long been a custom—practically a cliché—for lesbian couples to remain friends after a breakup. That phenomenon might stem partly from a sense of scarcity: people in small, oppressed communities can't afford to make enemies with each other...I think there's more. A habit of keeping former lovers in the family stems from an important vision, with impact far beyond the lesbian community—a recognition that relationships rarely evolve or dissolve in clear-cut ways.... Still, we have no words, let alone models, for

---

* Anndee Hochman, *Everyday Acts & Small Subversions: Women Reinventing Family, Community and Home* (Portland, OR: Eighth Mountain Press, 1994), pp. 140-141.

maintaining relationships as they shift course. Exist-
ing terms always use the past as a reference—"ex-
lover," "former partner"—while failing to articulate
what the relationship means now.*

Anne's years as part of Mischief Mime, the feminist acting troupe of two which she had cofounded, had given me access to a lot of women doing feminist theater, women's music,
and dyke comedy, so when I joined the Women's Week committee, I knew I had something to contribute. This confidence
was welcome, as opposed to my perpetual insecurity as a first-
year architectural graduate student.

The Women's Week meetings were held on the sixth floor
of Newman Library. Every Wednesday afternoon at 5:00, a dozen
or so women sat in cushy executive swivel chairs at a large
polished conference table, surrounded by wide glass windows,
discussing the feminist issues we barely whispered about outside that room on campus. We programmed an impressive bit
of radical entertainment and education for conservative Virginia
Tech, and I, meanwhile, checked out the obvious lesbians for
romantic promise and made mental notes about potential
friends.

Rebecca Wight fell into the latter category. A graduate of
Virginia Tech employed selling linen service all over southwest
Virginia, she was in a long-term, live-in relationship with a man.
Rebecca was a dark-skinned, dark-eyed, dark-haired woman; I
later learned that her mother was Puerto Rican and her father
Iranian and Western European. She was high energy, always
dashing. I found her attractive, theoretically, but dismissed any
potential romance: She was Heterosexual and Attached.

In the spring, during Women's Week itself, Rebecca offered
to help when I needed to transport the musician for the final
concert; I was producing that event. I appreciated her support,
but it never occurred to me that I was being given any signals.

Heterosexual. Attached. That summer, when she sent me a postcard from a South American adventure, I was surprised by the gesture. Our friendship seemed so casual.

We rarely saw each other the following fall and winter, my second year at Virginia Tech. I was invited to her house for dinner with three other lesbians once, but besides that, we hardly ran into each other. I had a scheduling conflict on Wednesday afternoons that semester, so I couldn't make most Women's Week '87 committee meetings. I did hear via the grapevine that Rebecca had left her long-term relationship and had started graduate school at Tech in the College of Business.

She and I went out in the same small group of people a couple of times as spring came, and I noticed that my attention had become very focused on her. And I noticed that it was mutual. I still hesitated to pursue this by now undeniable interest, not wanting to be caught in the often sticky web of a straight woman coming out. At this point in my life, I had no desire to be part of anybody's "experiment."

Caution made me miss some overt cues, but after she rested her hand on my thigh during a conversation at a Women's Week committee party, I finally grilled a mutual friend.

"What's the story with Rebecca?" I asked Janet. "Is she open to a relationship with a woman? Is she really all the way separated from Wayne? Does she like me?"

I pried, not knowing then that Rebecca had recently been pressing the same friend for the dish on me. In an effort to be honorable, Janet gave only sparse but encouraging information.

I took the leap when we returned to classes after spring break. I called on a Saturday and asked her if she wanted to go to the late showing of *Harold and Maude* with me. It turned out she already had plans for a movie earlier that evening, but said she would go to both. Two movies in one night? That must mean something, I thought. After a little discussion we decided we wouldn't go to the movie anyway, but at her suggestion, planned to meet for breakfast the next morning.

The restaurant was crowded. Conversation over our coffee and home fries *con* salsa was a little awkward, filled with bits about our lives but not the real topic. Afterward, we went outdoors on the slope near the edge of campus to sit in the early spring sunlight before returning to interminable schoolwork. I had known that given a chance of privacy, I would spill the beans about being attracted to her if I didn't get any contradictory signals during breakfast. I hadn't, but I still needed to take a deep breath before I told Rebecca that I had a crush on her.

She had a crush on me too. I was elated. I wanted a lot to fall in love with Rebecca, and I had her permission to do so. In the course of daily life I spent as much time daydreaming about her as I possibly could. Months after our first night of making love, the feelings still took my breath away.

It was a relationship destined by circumstance to be full of separations. Almost simultaneous with its beginning, I was notified that I had received a fellowship to do research for my thesis at the Technion in Haifa, Israel.

Nonetheless, Rebecca and I spent a sweet spring together. During Women's Week '87, Satya, then fifteen, came down to Blacksburg for the final concert. I spent part of the weekend on the same hill where Rebecca and I first acknowledged our attraction to each other helping Satya to master quadratic equations. She and Rebecca met that weekend, and I was happy to have my Ithaca and Blacksburg worlds mingle.

Since my home base was Ithaca, I returned there for the summer to earn money and prepare for the trip to Israel. The preceding fall, Anne had begun a relationship with Gina, which, by the summer, was firmly established. The dynamics between the three of us were awkward, but we all struggled to overcome them. Gina and I spent time together talking as openly as we could about the weird feelings, assuring each other we were not trying to rid the other person of their place in Anne's life. Anne continued to make me a priority and rearranged her schedule to spend a lot of time with me. We discussed having Satya come stay with me in Israel for part of the year. My dating Rebecca did not change that, and despite my reticence to fully embrace Anne's familial vision, I would never have made a major life decision without first talking with her. Although I had a sense that the family constellation might change someday, I wasn't yet sure how; Rebecca and I weren't nearly ready for such planning.

The years of nonmonogamy and sexual confusion with Anne added to the promise and bliss of the new relationship with Rebecca. We took every opportunity to spend time together and managed much Blacksburg-Ithaca travel, including some meetings in between. Despite the distance, we continued to grow closer.

I was occasionally aware that Rebecca was struggling with coming out. Most of the time, however, her comfort with both me and a lesbian lifestyle made me forget that this was her first relationship with a woman. It was only after returning to Ithaca from Israel in February that I grasped the extent of her struggle with homophobia: His name was Tony. Word of him had not surfaced in the long letters Rebecca sent me in Haifa, nor did she mention him in our wonderful BITNET conversations during the six months I was away.

Though Tony didn't last too long, it was a devastating situation to come home to. Rebecca had lost track of me in the months I was away. I was very hurt, but I loved her and wanted our relationship to continue. I fought for her. I saw Rebecca's behavior in the context of homophobia and insecurity, and when we talked about it, she did too. It was one of her wonderful qualities—a willingness to self-reflect and admit what was going on.

I was a bit cautious about placing my full trust in her, but overall felt open and ready to move forward. I had returned from Israel too late to start the spring semester at Tech, so I was waiting in Ithaca for a few months, scrambling to make money at odd jobs. Rebecca was exploring doctoral programs in Organizational Development.

I was pained once again when she chose not to apply to Cornell. But on one trip we took together that spring, Rebecca looked into Penn State and SUNY Buffalo. Then, more and more, she began to seriously consider location as a factor in applying to schools. She stopped investigating programs on the West Coast, even giving up one in Oregon in which she had been intensely interested. We both knew that our economic and emotional resources couldn't sustain a bicoastal relationship, and I had deep roots in upstate New York. We talked about how I was not certain I was going to return to Ithaca, but I was very reluctant to consider the West Coast. Rebecca finally was accepted at and chose Penn State.

In the homestretch of her master's thesis, and swamped with schoolwork, she managed to make time for me to come for a long visit in Blacksburg. I reconnected to my community at Tech, getting ready to return in the fall. As Rebecca wrote me in a postcard in late April: "We've ripped out a few thorny weeds and the flowers we planted last summer are blooming again...."

Two weeks after that visit, we met to go camping in Pennsylvania.

˒ TWO ˒

In the helicopter, I knew only my internal hysteria about Rebecca. I hardly spoke to the E.M.T. All my thoughts were about my lover, waiting for help in the woods. While I communicated almost nothing, I took everything in. My senses were swollen with adrenaline. After landing on a pad at the hospital twenty-eight minutes later, white-coated people appeared through the open door of the helicopter. As I was unloaded and wheeled toward the hospital, flat on my back, a part of me noticed the cool air and the night sky.

Uniforms alongside a moving stretcher. Vital statistics. White...female...thirty-one...gunshot victim. The scene was entirely unoriginal; I'd seen all of this on TV. A large, brightly lit room appeared, with antiseptic-looking machines on every shelf. There was something bizarre about all the emergency treatment, because the person on the stretcher had been taking care of herself for over six hours. *What exactly is the rush?* I thought. I had no idea, then, that my body had managed to stabilize itself despite having five extra holes ripped in it, four of them in the head and neck.

The trauma unit staff virtually pounced on my body. A steady rain of hands, all at once, pulse-taking, reflex-checking, muscle-probing. They took my blood pressure and blood type, inserted a catheter. Nurses and technicians appeared near my head, told me their names and what they were about to do, then disappeared from view. I could feel the barrage of procedures, but what I saw were the beige walls and ceiling.

I thought about Rebecca. She was a long way away. Travel by foot, ambulance, and helicopter separated us. I imagined her in the woods, near the small trees, a bullet somewhere in her torso. A punctured lung? Maybe that could explain her wheezing, her collapsing.

A very beautiful, young, white male nurse with steady blue eyes, named Mark, spent any free moments holding my hand, listening to me, meeting my gaze, and explaining what was happening. I told him I was thinking that maybe Rebecca had a punctured lung.

Mark said, "We have two lungs." He said it matter-of-factly, without a rise or a drop in his voice. When he became one of the unseen pairs of hands again, I held on to the vision of Rebecca breathing from one undamaged lung, under the sleeping bag, until help reached her.

Mark came back often. A bit later I said to him, "If they find out that Rebecca is dead, please don't tell me tonight. I don't want to find out from strangers."

Two ear, nose, and throat—E.N.T.—specialists introduced themselves and began examining my wounds. They were young, residents maybe. One was a woman, and at first I thought that she was a nurse and Mark was a doctor. She and the other E.N.T. specialist seemed puzzled by my injuries. My arm was simple: One doctor slid a piece of fine wire into the hole at the front of my arm and it emerged out the back. It was my head and neck that were more complicated. The doctors didn't know where the "entry" and "exit" wounds were. I may have known for hours that I had been shot, but it was only then, with those two words, that I began to comprehend—bullets.

It was approaching midnight. The flood of adrenaline had

begun to recede, and I was more and more aware of exhaustion and pain. Particularly pain.

An older Black man in a priest's collar came to my side. I told him that I was Jewish.

The chaplain explained that it was his job simply to notify whomever I wanted of what had happened. I asked that he call Anne, and gave him two numbers, one at her home on Wood Street in Ithaca, and the other at Gina's house in Freeville. The chaplain suggested that I might also want to call my parents. I was reluctant. Who wants to tell their parents that they and their lesbian lover have been shot in the woods? I told him that my father had already had several heart attacks.

"I'll be very gentle," the priest assured me. He was right. They should know. What if I died? I gave him my parents' number in New York City.

The head surgeon arrived to examine me. After looking at an x-ray of my head, Dr. Weigand pushed gently on the back of my skull.

"Does it hurt here?"

"Yes." I thought about it and then said, "I think I was shot in the head." I sensed the residents' mounting anxiety with the discovery of yet another wound. Their faces were calm, but their eyes said: *How many does she have?* Dr. Weigand was professional, the look on his face undisturbed, and very caring.

"Can you make a fist with your right hand?" he asked. I could, and he seemed surprised. I knew I would be able to because I had stopped just before leaving the campsite and wiggled all my fingers. I had distinctly thought, while staring at the palms of my hands, "At least I can still be an architect."

"What happened to your tongue?"

"I don't know. I guess I bit it," I replied. Up until that point, I hadn't noticed anything wrong with my tongue, though it was lacerated raw. I told Dr. Weigand that I couldn't swallow at all and that my ears hurt a lot. "Mostly I spit out when I was walking."

I had spewed blood and saliva and hard bits from my mouth every few minutes for several hours and, after he questioned me about my tongue, I suddenly connected that nauseating experience with the fact that I had been shot in the face. Those hard bits had been my teeth, shattered by the impact of a bullet. The team of doctors, who could see the insides of my mouth, were not surprised when I related this realization.

The clergyman returned in the midst of the exam and told me he had struck out on all counts. Were there other numbers where these people could be reached? I gave him Kris and Ellen's number, long-time friends of mine and Anne's who lived a few blocks from Anne's house. I also remembered that my parents might be at their weekend apartment in Atlantic City. I didn't know the number, but the priest assured me that he could locate them by calling Information, and left to try.

The two residents and Dr. Weigand began to discuss whether or not they needed to do an extra diagnostic test to make sure that they had located all of my injuries, something about hyper-filling my arteries and watching for blood to spurt out of any undetected wounds. From the moment my treatment began, I had demanded to know the reason for each tiny procedure done to me. Mark had answered many questions. If choices weren't offered, I created them, at least in my mind. When the doctors told me that I had to swallow some mysteriously named liquid in order for them to take more x-rays, I asked if it was radioactive.

After that question, Dr. Weigand gently cupped my head in his hands, placing a palm protectively on either side of my face, his fingers near my neck. He made sure I was looking at him and said slowly, "You have gunshot wounds in your neck." He paused to let the words sink in. "These are extraordinary circumstances, and I really think we need to do this diagnostic procedure."

Gunshot wounds in your neck. A wave of comprehension swept through me, and I understood. I was in a trauma center in Hershey, Pennsylvania, transported there by helicopter. I had been shot. It was not just a matter of stitching me up. I had entry and exit wounds, in my neck and head.

Power to control my world had shattered with the bullets, and then power over my own body had slipped away from me bit by bit, beginning in Chambersburg when I realized that I could not lead the rescue team back to Rebecca. I didn't want to, but I had to trust them.

"Okay," I said. The doctors left the room to consult, leaving one or two other trauma unit staff to monitor and wait with me. Tubes, sterile instruments. Mark's blue eyes. Terror.

Where was Rebecca?

A nurse appeared against the background of beeping machines and cabinets and told me a state police officer was there, and he needed to speak with me.

Denny Beaver wasn't in uniform. Throughout the investigation, we never saw him or his counterpart from Adams County, Don Blevins, in uniform; state police detectives wear plainclothes. Trooper Beaver was only a darkish shirt covering broad shoulders at the foot of the bed, with a clean-cut face, and some name that didn't register.

He introduced himself. Apologies, procedure, queries. I cooperated, but it felt meaningless. One more fucking person asking me to tell them the same stupid things. Besides, the officer in Chambersburg had asked these questions. Why didn't this cop already know this stuff? Shot by a stream. Had seen a skinny, straggly guy with a gun earlier in the day. He asked Rebecca for cigarettes. Had never met him before. A stranger. Had seen no one else. Rebecca couldn't walk. Left Rebecca. Walked out of the woods. No one would have any cause to shoot us. No enemies. He left.

He left the room without telling me that the state police

had already found Rebecca's body.

He left the room without me telling him that the state police had just found the body of my *lover.*

The priest came back. He had reached Ellen and Kris and also my parents. He had told them that no one could see me until morning because soon I would be in surgery that would last all night. Several people whom Kris and Ellen contacted had called back, he told me, including Anne and my close friend Nancie, who lived in Philadelphia.

"She wants to come," he said of Nancie. "What shall I tell her?"

"Tell her yes," I said.

The doctors returned, having decided on the least invasive diagnostic route. Even though the paths of the bullets confused them, they felt confident that they understood my injuries. I was taken out of the trauma unit and wheeled to the x-ray room.

The table on which they laid me could rotate in all directions, like a gyroscope but flat. After my body was secured to it, they moved it from horizontal to almost vertical for the best view of my upper body, and the computer generated an x-ray picture on its terminal.

I had to gag and spit up and force myself to try, and try again, to swallow the radioactive liquid which could reveal the hole in my throat. The adrenaline that had masked the pain had faded completely by this time. Suction had relieved me of having to swallow for the past few hours, but now, while the technicians and Dr. Wiegand were very supportive and patient, it was only me who could choke down the cup of chemicals.

I was crying, bloody, and exhausted. It hurt every time I swallowed. After each struggle, I could see the picture on the screen, liquid spurting out where it didn't belong. The machine clicked, making the image permanent.

When the procedure was over, I was wheeled into the hall. I pictured Rebecca, injured but surviving with a punctured lung in Pine Grove Furnace State Park. I held on to that image, and imagining her made me not give up on my own survival. I think I might have died then, or in surgery, if I had let myself believe what I already half-knew: Rebecca was dead.

Dr. Weigand asked me to sign a release that acknowledged the possibility of death during surgery, but I was only briefly frightened. He told me that after all I'd been through, with the level of stabilization my body had managed to achieve, the probability of death was low. Besides, what choice did I have? I let him know that I didn't have health insurance, and he reassured me he was not concerned.

When they finally began to administer the anesthesia, I was grateful. I wanted a break. I hurt all over and I didn't know where Rebecca was. It was awful. I wanted to not be conscious of just how horrible it was.

The anesthesiologist put me under at 2:00 A.M. The first team of specialists slit the flesh in my neck, creating an opening that would heal into a thin, five-inch-long scar. They stretched layers of skin apart to reach the postage-stamp-sized hole in the back of my esophagus which had been ripped open by bullet fragments, and they sewed the wound shut. They examined my vocal chords, which were entirely undamaged.

A second team of surgeons took over to deal with the more straightforward bullet wounds. They sewed up the lacerations in my tongue, and the holes in my neck, face, and arm. Fragments of bullet were removed from my mouth and throat, having stopped fractions of an inch short of my spinal column. Had my two back left molars not been in the way, an intact bullet would have ripped into my spine, and the .22 inch slug of lead would have destroyed the third vertebrae.

＞

Friday the thirteenth always made Don Blevins nervous. He said it was when kids decided to pull some stupid stunt or regular people got squirrely. At 10:00 P.M. on Friday, May 13, 1988, Trooper Blevins only had an hour left on his shift. Don was a tall man, with chestnut hair and a broad face. He had been a criminal investigator for ten years. He was having a cup of coffee in the shift supervisor's office when the phone buzzed. It was the dispatcher. She had been contacted by the Cumberland County state police about an emergency.

Less than an hour later, Don was in the middle of eighty-two thousand acres of timberland. He hadn't changed out of his jacket and tie and dress shoes. Two eight-person search parties—with police officers, an EMT, a firefighter, and a forest ranger in each—had driven as close as they could in four-wheel-drive jeeps to the area on the map indicated by the victim who had made it out of the woods. One party was to the east of the area the woman had circled, and one to the west. Five miles separated the two. Don was in one unit, but supervising both.

Don's search party parked, turned on high-powered flashlights and a two-way radio, and started walking. The officers called the victim's name constantly. It was pitch black, and the path was often blocked by fallen trees. Much of it was uphill.

One hour and two and one-half miles later, they met the other search party, neither having seen a sign of Rebecca Wight. They split up again, walking back in the directions they had come.

＞

If anyone heard the phone ringing at 230 Wood Street, they decided to let whoever it was call back in the morning.

Anne awoke to pounding at the back door. She was sleeping with Gina on a mattress on the floor, having given her father, who was visiting, her bed for the night. She went downstairs without turning on the lights.

Hard, quick knocks. "Annie." Anne recognized Kris's voice calling her name in a loud whisper. "Annie." It was after midnight, and something was clearly wrong.

When Anne opened the door Kris was shaking. She came into the dark kitchen and said, "Claudia's been shot in the head and they can't find Rebecca." She said it twice. "Claudia's been shot in the head and they can't find Rebecca."

It wouldn't go in. Claudia's been shot. Kris wasn't making it up, but Anne could not make it be real. She stood frozen. Kris was still shaking.

Anne whispered, "How?"

Kris told her that she had gotten a call from the hospital when they couldn't reach Anne at Wood Street.

Unable to get a sentence out of her mouth, Anne only managed, "What? Who?"

They were speaking very softly; everyone in the house was asleep. Kris told Anne that Claudia was in Hershey Medical Center in Pennsylvania in surgery, and the police were looking for Rebecca. That was all she knew.

"We have to go," Anne said.

"Ellen's calling Fran and Judy, too," Kris said.

They planned to meet at Kris's house, then hugged each other and Kris left.

Anne went back upstairs to Gina. The thought that if she just went back to sleep, it would all go away passed through her mind. Her heart was beating fast as she spoke. "Claudia's been shot. She's in surgery at Hershey Medical Center. They can't find Rebecca."

She and Gina discussed what to do. Anne wished she could be at Hershey that second. She realized she needed clothes, money, needed to make arrangements. Anne pushed a picture of Claudia's face with bullet holes in it out of her head. Gina agreed to stay and tell Satya when she woke up. They got dressed, woke up Ruth, their housemate, and Anne sat down to call Claudia's parents.

Rhoda Brenner's voice was shaky. Anne didn't know what to say to her. She wished she could comfort her, could offer real encouragement. Claudia's parents didn't have any additional information, even though the hospital had reached them directly.

Anne then called Hershey, but the person on the other end of the phone refused to tell her anything. She called again a few minutes later, pretending to be Claudia's sister, but when the call was transferred to the chaplain, he would give her no new facts and questioned her with suspicion. "Have you called your mother? Your mother has been contacted. She will tell you everything that we know."

Anne realized that the hospital had no way of knowing who she was; she could be the person or one of the persons who shot Claudia, for all they knew. They were probably instructed not to give out any information. It occurred to her that if she had been able to put an acceptable label on her relationship with Claudia—spouse, parent of their child, ex-husband—she might have been treated with less distrust. She gave up.

Before leaving for Pennsylvania, Anne woke Satya and said, "Claudia's been in an accident. I'm going over to Kris and Ellen's. I'll tell you about it later." Then she left her daughter and father to sleep through the night. When Anne, Gina, and Ruth arrived at Kris and Ellen's house, the pair were already sitting in the living room with Judy and Fran, turning over the little knowledge they had. They all spoke frantically but quietly, as Ellen and Kris's toddler was asleep in the next room.

Who should go? We need a map. Who's going to watch the kids? What car should we take? Should we take two cars? How long is the drive? What if we have to stay longer? Someone should bring food. After half an hour, Gina and Ruth, maybe because they were not as close to Claudia as the other five women, cut it off.

"Just go. It doesn't matter; someone will take care of the kids. Just go now." Anne, Kris, and Ruth set out for the five-hour trip to Hershey, Pennsylvania, with Ruth driving. It was after 1:00 A.M.

The three women alternated between talking nonstop—
*Were Rebecca and Claudia both shot? If they were both shot
and somebody found Claudia, why didn't they find Rebecca?
Maybe only Claudia was shot. How did someone find her?
Maybe Rebecca ran*—and reminding each other that their endless speculation was ridiculous. Stupid. They didn't know. They'd
have to wait until they got to Hershey to find out. But in the
ensuing silence, their minds careened wildly, fixing on possibilities both hopeful and terrible. No version of the story to
explain Rebecca's absence seemed plausible. Then discipline
would collapse and one of them would begin to conjecture out
loud, the others would join in, and soon they would have to
quiet each other again.

They tried listening to the radio, but couldn't. It was 240
miles to Hershey, Pennsylvania. The hospital had said it was
unlikely that Claudia would die in surgery, but what would she
be like afterward? They knew it was a good sign that before the
operation she was coherent enough to tell them phone numbers. Ruth drove the whole way. Once in a while, someone looked
at the map. It grew light.

‚

The two search parties of police began pacing away from
each other a second time. Within one hundred yards, an officer
in the other group radioed Don's party that they had found the
campsite. Don and the officers in his group ran back. When they
arrived, Don waved everybody off. He reached for Rebecca's neck
under the blue sleeping bag and felt for a pulse. There was none.

A few of the half-dozen officers stayed with her body all
night. They could not bring it out until morning because the
scene had to remain undisturbed until they could photograph
it. Under the early morning sky, they took pictures of the entire
area. More police officers returned, and they searched in the
bed of moss under the tarp, along the stream, in Claudia and

Rebecca's backpacks. They walked through the surrounding woods, their arms spread out on each side, fingertip to fingertip, each examining their column of terrain for clues. Some had to crawl through laurel thicket. Eighty-two feet away from the bloody tarp by the stream, they found a jackknife, eight empty bullet shell casings, a pair of sunglasses, a blue knit cap with animal hair on it, two cigarette lighters, and twenty-five rounds of live .22 caliber ammunition. When Don lay down near the spot, he could look back through a "window" in the thicket and see the officers where he had told them to lie down in the lush, green spot where Rebecca and Claudia had been.

➤

Gina had fallen back asleep for a few hours. Ellen had promised to call if she got any word from the three who were traveling to Hershey, and Gina had said she would do the same. When the ringing phone woke her, the clock read just after 6:00 A.M. Gina answered it expecting news from Anne or Ellen.

Don Blevins, after identifying himself as an officer with the Adams County state police, wanted to know to whom he was speaking and what Gina's relationship to Rebecca was. Instead of explaining that she was Rebecca's lover's ex-lover's lover, Gina told him that she had met Rebecca a few times, that she knew Claudia had been shot in the head and that Rebecca was missing.

The detective explained that he had gotten this phone number from another officer who had gotten it from Claudia Brenner, and that he was trying to gather some more information about Rebecca: What her sister's name was, where they lived, where their parents were, and was their last name W-I-G-H-T or W-H-I-T-E? Gina was able to give him Rebecca and Evelyn's address and telephone number—Rebecca and her sister lived together—since Claudia had left it for them the last time she went for a visit. Gina didn't know anything about their parents, but told him that she was pretty sure the spelling was the former.

Trooper Blevins said, "You do know that Rebecca is deceased?"

"No," said Gina. The room was lit yellow by the dawn. "I didn't know that."

"Yes. We found her body at 11:40 P.M. last night at the campsite."

"Oh."

Trooper Blevins wanted to know if there was anyone down in Virginia who was close to Evelyn from whom she might better receive the news about her sister than a uniformed officer. Gina's guts twisted. But she said she would contact, or get someone to contact, one of Claudia's friends at Tech who knew Evelyn. Mechanically, Gina said good-bye. After they hung up, Gina immediately picked the phone back up to call Ellen.

⋆

Anne, Kris, and Ruth arrived at the hospital at about 6:00 A.M. Everything felt unreal to Anne—the gravel underfoot in the parking lot, the blue sky, the heavy Emergency Room doors. The lobby was typical: impersonal, carpeted, the furniture grouped.

The three of them went to the receptionist and said that they were friends of Claudia Brenner. She told them that Claudia had gone into surgery and would be out soon if she wasn't out already.

"What about Rebecca?" they asked.

She said she didn't have any information about Rebecca.

"Have the police found her?"

No information.

"Do you know anything?"

She said she couldn't tell them anything about Rebecca, and that she was sorry. Anne felt like the receptionist knew more than she was saying. If Rebecca had been shot and had been found, she would probably be at the hospital.

"Not even whether a person named Rebecca Wight has been admitted to this hospital?"

"No," said the woman, looking nervous, "there is no patient by that name."

The receptionist glanced down a long hall where a doctor was walking toward them. He came through the glass doors and the receptionist told him who they were. He greeted them warmly, introducing himself as Dr. Weigand, one of the surgeons who had just been working on Claudia. He looked tired.

Dr. Weigand said Claudia was out of surgery. She was alive and fine.

Anne waited for the "but," thinking he would say she was blind, or her face was torn up, or her brain had been damaged. He told them Claudia's gunshot wounds had brought her very close to death or paralysis.

"A miracle," he said. She had been shot five times, four bullets in the head and neck. Each one came dangerously close to destroying something crucial: her spinal chord, her vocal chords, her brain, her eyesight. A quarter of an inch in one direction or another, or a slightly different inclination of her head, and she surely would have died or been severely damaged. But she was fine.

Anne wanted to cry but still couldn't. The doctor kept telling them she was fine. She would have no lasting problems. She would recover fully.

"What about Rebecca?" Anne asked.

His face went blank and he glanced at the receptionist. He said he didn't have any information about Rebecca.

"Did they find her?"

He was silent.

Anne got angry. "We are very close friends of Claudia's and we drove all the way from Ithaca in the middle of the night and you won't tell us anything about Rebecca at all? Where would she be if she's not here?"

Silence. Anne didn't know what else to say. They wouldn't have brought Claudia here and taken Rebecca somewhere else.

Finally the receptionist said, "I'm sorry to tell you that Rebecca is dead. The state police found her body late last night."

Kris turned around, saying she felt sick. She went out to the parking lot. Anne couldn't feel anything. Someone killed Rebecca, she thought. *Rebecca died because someone shot her.* Anne went into a kind of numb and distant panic.

Dr. Weigand said that Claudia was in the recovery room and Anne, Kris, and Ruth could see her soon. He told them she didn't know about Rebecca yet. He left. The receptionist said she was sorry. Ruth and Anne sat down in the hard foam chairs. Kris came back in. She was shaking again. They waited.

,

It was about 7:20 A.M. when Karen heard the phone ringing at the other end of her trailer. Since she'd been out the night before—Friday the thirteenth—to a party in Roanoke, she just pulled the covers over her head. The machine picked up after four rings, and she heard her own outgoing message, then two beeps. Who in the hell could it be? she wondered.

Beep. "Karen, this is Ellen in Ithaca. There's been an emergency. Claudia and Rebecca were camping and were in an accident—"

Karen sprang out of bed to pick up the phone.

"Hello, this is Karen, what kind of accident? They were camping? They were shot!? Claudia's being operated on? Rebecca's dead!? You've got to be kidding—" But her light-headed, nauseous body knew that the woman on the other end of the line wasn't joking. "I've got to tell Evelyn? Oh my God. Why can't the police do it—" Then immediately Karen realized it would be better if Evelyn heard it from her.

After she hung up, Karen put her head down between her

knees to keep from fainting. She called her friend Pam and managed to tell her what happened. They decided to go tell Evelyn together; Pam would come pick Karen up. Pam was housesitting twenty minutes away.

The wait was torturously long. Karen went outside, then in. Outside, inside. It was a beautiful spring morning in Blacksburg. Humid and misty already, with the promise of a hot day. The dogwoods that lined the road up to her trailer were blooming. She couldn't stand still and finally went out to her mailbox to wait for Pam there. Karen talked to herself in her anxiety: What could they say to Evelyn?

❦

Anne's voice saying my name. That's the first thing I heard as I regained consciousness. I think I was waiting until I knew Anne was there to come fully out from under the anesthesia. She walked across the room to my bed. She said my name. I said her name.

"Where's Rebecca?" I asked her when she reached the side of my bed.

Through the mass of oxygen mask and tubes covering my face, of which I was totally unconscious, I could see Anne's eyes.

"She's gone Claudia. She's gone. She died."

"No." I turned my head very slowly from side to side. "No. No." Please make it not be true. She had never moved from the place where I left her. She had never spoken another word.

I asked Anne again. She repeated her answer.

"She's gone, Claudia. She died."

Minutes went by. I cried. I motioned Anne to come closer. She bent her head down near my face. In a whisper, I said to Anne: "He saw us."

Anne stayed with me, holding my hand as I came fully awake, and was with me almost constantly all through that first day. Eventually I became aware of the oxygen mask and the machine with the constant beeps that was monitoring my heartbeat. Anne put the suction tube to my lips every few minutes so that I would not have to swallow. The nurses came with shots of morphine. I didn't really care about any of it. Rebecca was dead. Everything else was irrelevant. I spoke in a whisper to Anne, who delivered my words to others who came into the room. In the next several hours, Kris, Ruth, my parents, and Nancie all visited for a few minutes. To each of them, I said, "Rebecca's dead."

Denny Beaver came back that day also. I didn't remember him from the night before until he reintroduced himself. He had greying hair, cut short and combed straight back from a receding widow's peak, a young-looking face, blue eyes, and was clean shaven. He looked like an ex-high school football hero-turned-coach.

His persistent questioning did not come off as "cop-ish" or tough, just plain and honest. Despite his rather gentle demeanor, I gave him nothing new, speaking through Anne, deeply in my grief. I still said nothing about my relationship with Rebecca.

I didn't even consider telling him. It was second nature to hide being a lesbian, especially from a police officer, or any person with power over my life.

My self-protection as a lesbian never stopped functioning, even in the depths of this tragedy. While still bleeding, while they were the only help I had, I withheld from the police both my relationship with Rebecca and what I knew had been the motivation for the attack. I continued to do so when the direct threat to my life was past. Far from feeling uncooperative, I withheld the information out of terror. Someone had just shot us for being lesbians. Why would I allow yet one more unknown man to know that fact?

So it was only to my friends that I said: *He saw us.* Those three words gave all the essential information. He saw that we were lesbians. He shot us because we were lesbians. I didn't even have to wonder if there was some other motivation. I just knew. We all did.

I didn't yet know this act of brutality had a name. The term *antigay violence* was not in my vocabulary. But I knew what had happened to me was not random.

In those first days, an attorney friend of ours foresaw a legal tidal wave: a murder, an attempted murder, two lesbians, a death-penalty state, a bias-related crime. Susan predicted that the proceedings would not be cut and dried. She could imagine how the case would look down the road: The murderer, if the case was even fully investigated and the police caught him, would be given probation for killing my lover. This was not paranoia, and cases I subsequently read confirmed Susan's foreboding.

In the early 1980s, two high school seniors in Washington, D.C. were given four hundred hours of community service after savagely beating, nearly to death, a gay man whom they had invited to a party. In another case, Texas Judge Jack Hampton excused his light sentencing of the murderer of two gay men with: "I put prostitutes and queers at the same level...and I'd be hard put to give somebody life for killing a prostitute."*

We didn't know if sodomy was illegal in Pennsylvania, and if it was, what the implications of "criminal sodomites" being shot would be. But we did fear that whether or not it was illegal, the police might do an 180-degree turnaround if they found out I was a lesbian. Susan began to look into the possibility of hiring a lawyer for me.

My fear and terror were multilayered and relentless.

---

*Kevin T. Berrill and Gregory M. Herek, editors, *Hate Crimes: Confronting Violence Against Lesbians and Gay Men* (Newbury Park, CA: Sage Publications, 1992), p. 294.

· THREE ·

Evelyn had been visiting a friend and returned home to the apartment she shared with Rebecca. The next morning, Saturday, hard knocking on the door woke her up. It was 8:00 A.M. She heard Karen and Pam's voices calling her name as they walked in her unlocked door. She came out of her room naked and surprised, squinting at their faces without her contacts in.

Pam blurted out something unintelligible. It sounded like she was crying, though Evelyn could not see her face clearly.

Then Karen said very slowly, "Rebecca and Claudia were camping and there was a terrible accident. Rebecca is dead."

The three women held on to each other as Karen told Evelyn everything she knew about the shooting. They stood, shaking, until Evelyn left them and went to get dressed. Karen and Pam stayed in the kitchen, while Evelyn looked at all of her clothes. Deciding what to wear seemed too remote after having just been told her sister was dead.

As Karen and Pam made what seemed like a million phone calls, and later as Evelyn sat in a car for the drive to her family near D.C., she began to memorize images of Rebecca.

Evelyn also thought about what might happen with the police. She worried about telling her father that Rebecca was a lesbian. Of the three daughters, their father had been particularly close to Rebecca. The shock of her death would be painful enough, and Evelyn knew that he would not be able to understand that his daughter had been shot while camping with a woman lover. It was better to wait, wait until she had a chance to talk to Claudia.

They took two cars: Evelyn was driven by her friend, Jim; Karen and Pam were in the other car. At the rest stops, Karen was afraid to get out of the car, afraid that someone might shoot them.

They drove to Judy's house first. Evelyn's sister was surprised to see them all—in fact, she was expecting Rebecca and Claudia that very day for a birthday gathering. Pam and Karen stood around uncomfortably as Evelyn told Judy what had happened. Judy sat down hard, her face blank.

Karen and Pam headed back to Blacksburg. Evelyn and Judy, with Jim, drove the few minutes to their father and stepmother's house to break the news. Before they arrived, Evelyn reminded everyone to watch what they said about Rebecca and Claudia.

After twenty-four hours, my face was finally free of the oxygen mask. There was dense pain in my neck and head, beeping machines, and morphine shots. Rebecca was dead. Kris and Ruth returned to Ithaca. Gina, Satya, Fran, and Ellen arrived.

When doctors came to the intensive care unit on Sunday, they were satisfied with my physical progress and wanted to transfer me, that day, to the less acute critical care unit. Because intensive care means the patient might die at any moment, I had been permitted twenty-four-hour visitation. In critical care, the patient is deemed stabilized, and round-the-clock visitors are not allowed. There simply is not enough physical space, the staff told us.

"Then I'm not going," I said. "I'll stay here."

Having my friends with me at all times was not negotiable.

There was not a chance that I was going to be put somewhere where I had to be alone. I was too terrified. Anne and Nancie and my parents firmly backed up my refusal. It was a first step on a long road of self-advocacy.

The attending hospital psychiatrist, Dr. Noori, had visited the day before, checking in and making sure that I was not considering suicide. That visit seemed to be standard operating procedure at Hershey for survivors of trauma. I was many things, but suicidal was not one of them, and the previous day's visit had been relatively unmemorable. On Sunday, however, he returned. Nancie's partner had contacted a colleague, a psychiatrist at Penn State, who had called with a friendly professional suggestion for Dr. Noori about this case. That roundabout connection greased the wheels enough for Dr. Noori to visit again and give me a formal diagnosis of Post-Traumatic Stress Disorder.

Though I had heard of the "Vietnam vet syndrome" before, it did not occur to me to label my feelings with that name or any other. All I knew was that I did not want to be alone. Anne later described the face of the person she saw when she first entered the intensive care unit: colorless skin, literally grey, with eyes that showed a terror she had never seen before. The greyness passed as I healed and replaced the pints of lost blood, but the terror receded from my eyes much more slowly. My anxiety and pain were unbearable except with people whom I trusted most around me.

Dr. Noori's note to hospital staff prescribed constant company: "She should have friends around her whom she trusts at all times." Somewhere in the bureaucracy of the hospital administration it was decided the circumstances warranted that I have twenty-four-hour companionship. The rules were broken.

⁊

Denny spent much time in and out of the intensive and critical care units in the first few days after the shooting. He stayed for hours, talking with various members of my family. Though he was only one of many officers that the state of Pennsylvania assigned to the investigation, he had become the police department's prime contact with "the surviving witness." Anne later told me about his gentle but insistent questioning of her and everyone else he could talk to.

"How long have you known Claudia?" Denny asked Anne in the hall outside my room. "What's her relationship with her parents like? Is there anybody you can think of in Ithaca who might be angry at Claudia, or who might have been hurt by her? Is there anybody in Blacksburg who held a grudge against her or Rebecca? How is she feeling? When do you think she'll be ready to give us some more information?"

Anne talked a lot with him but had few answers. Denny rarely ran out of questions before Anne would leave to come and be with me.

Evelyn's journal entry from Sunday, May 15, read: "Food arrives. Last straw for me." She sat huddled under a coatrack outside the restaurant's women's bathroom, rocking back and forth. Judy, her father, stepmother, and stepbrothers were at a table in the restaurant, trying to eat. They had all just left the funeral home, a few blocks away in downtown Gettysburg, Pennsylvania.

Rebecca would not have wanted a church service, Evelyn had stressed. She was enraged that the funeral director would try to sell them an urn, or anything. The family had decided that Rebecca's body would be cremated and her ashes kept in an enameled vase her father had at home. They would arrange for their own memorial service.

Evelyn felt like she had been answering questions all day— the undertaker's questions, her family's questions, the police officers' questions. The Wights had gone first to the police station when they arrived in Gettysburg that morning. The investigators seemed to have no interest in talking to Judy or their stepbrothers, but had only spoken with Evelyn, her father, and stepmother. Her interview had lasted more than two hours, during which time Evelyn truthfully answered all of their mundane questions: "Where do you live?" "Do you know Claudia Brenner?" And she had evaded their probing questions: "What is the nature of the relationship between Claudia and Anne?" "How did Claudia and Rebecca know each other?" They put a lot of pressure on Evelyn. In exchange, she told them that she didn't trust them.

She was waiting to talk to Claudia. Her family was going home tonight, and the next day Jim was driving her up to Hershey.

⸙

The space was tight in critical care, as promised, with just enough room for a chair between the curtains separating the beds. One chair was all we needed, though. All night I held Nancie's or Anne's hand through the cold metal guard rail of the hospital bed.

The nurses had to change my sheets once, and when they lifted me, I became aware of the raw, five-inch slice in my neck. It felt like it was going to rip. "Be careful of my neck, be careful of my neck," I begged.

A guard had been posted outside the door to the critical care unit. The police officer had come and introduced himself in the morning, and occasionally made a sweep through the room and the nearby hall throughout the day. Having a guard outside my door, however, made me feel caged and watched, not more secure.

In the middle of the day, an unfamiliar man walked through the unit, emptying the trash. He terrified me, though I could not say why. He stopped throughout the room, picking up the can at the end of every bed and dumping it into the receptacle on the cart he pushed. When he got near my bed, he looked at me momentarily. I said nothing out loud but inside I screamed. He walked on, the back of his shirt hanging out of his pants. I later figured out that his ruddy complexion reminded me of the as yet nameless murderer.

After the struggle about visitation policies, I remained in critical care only twenty-four hours. The night passed, and on Monday I was moved to a regular private room on the fifth floor where I stayed for my remaining eight days at the hospital.

The entire time I was at Hershey, I believed that someone might kill me. A hidden gun in oversized clothing seemed not only conceivable, but logical. All strangers were suspect, particularly if they were male. Mark, the blue-eyed nurse who had talked me through my initial hours at the hospital, stopped up to visit. When he entered the room I didn't recognize him at first. Gina, who had been sitting with me, jumped up to confront him, sensing my fears. He looked hurt, but he was an unfamiliar man, and I was terrified.

This terror turned me into a control freak. I would insist that the clock on the windowsill be turned exactly—*Five degrees more to the left, no the left, the left!*—as I wanted it. *Don't set that there! Sit here, not there.* My family tolerated me, both loving me and making me feel completely safe, and also occasionally putting a foot down when I couldn't tell the difference between a need and an unwarranted need-to-control.

There were moments of panic for them, too. One day Ellen and Fran saw an unidentified man outside the hospital smoking and looking nervous. He was wearing grey sweatpants with a maroon stripe. So had the murderer. No one knew how sophisticated Rebecca's killer was. Would he track me to Hershey, walk in, and blow me away? The idea seemed entirely plausible.

Denny Beaver had eliminated the private guard when I was moved out of critical care, but had taken other precautions: The police told the press that I had been moved, not specifying that they meant only to the fifth floor. When the media reported that I had been transferred to a different hospital, neither the police nor Hershey corrected them. My hospital wristband read "Jane Doe." They tightened security, particularly on the fifth floor. One day, some hospital security guards who didn't know Denny interrogated him when he got off the elevator on the wrong floor and was wandering about.

I did not sleep much in the nights, listening to the bleeping of life support machines, dozing off and then jerking awake from morphine-induced sleep and nightmares. My family stayed with me in shifts, the ones not at the hospital sleeping at a nearby motel. I talked all the time—about the shooting, about Rebecca's death, about the fear and pain. Everything was raw; there was no softening with politeness or niceties. Nearly every waking moment was involved in processing the impossibility of Rebecca's death and my survival.

I obsessed about the dozens of decisions one makes all the time that are never supposed to become important. Important because of wishing that one of them would have been different enough to change the course of events. I finally consented to a prescription for sleeping pills, but the dull slumber they gave was worse than the haze of the morphine while I was awake.

⸸

Karen had received word on Sunday that it was okay to come up to Hershey and see Claudia. She had spent twenty-four hours almost nonstop on the phone, calling everyone in her own life, in Blacksburg, keeping in contact with people at the hospital. She talked to two professors, got her exams postponed, and drove up with Pam the next day.

It was Tuesday when Karen finally arrived. Evelyn got to the hospital at about the same time, and they went into Claudia's room together. Claudia had tubes going in and out of her; her eyes were stark and wide. Karen felt terrified under her skin, as she had almost continuously for the past four days.

Claudia told them the entire story of the shooting. A nurse had to interrupt the end of it to give her medication. Back at the hotel, Evelyn told Karen she had not been eating or sleeping, but both women slept some that night, and the next morning Evelyn described to Karen what she had dreamt:

Claudia and I and someone else are in the woods. They're cartoon woods, like in "Frosty the Snowman." We're laughing uproariously. Then Rebecca waltzes in, the way she always bounces and strides, dressed in jeans and a blue shirt. She leans up against a tree and starts laughing with us. Claudia and I and the other person telepathically agree to believe that she is there with us, and because we believe it, she is.

During the entire ten days of my hospital stay, my room was kept subdued and calm. One or two of my round-the-clock caregivers—Anne, Gina, Nancie, Ellen, Fran, my parents, Satya, and Karen—were with me at all times. No other visitors were permitted unless they were hospital staff or the police. No phone calls were made from my bedside.

Outside of my room, however, action was erupting. I knew only a handful of the thirty thousand residents of Ithaca personally, but a giant mobilization had begun to provide my family with everything they needed—money, information, automobiles, support. People sent meals to Hershey so that those who were taking care of me would not have to subsist on hospital cafeteria food. Other friends wanted to visit or just send good wishes, flowers, a card. The Family and Children's Service of Ithaca, a past employer of mine, established the Claudia Brenner Fund so that donations could be made to a single place. In less than a month, six thousand dollars was collected. Therapists, lawyers, doctors offered their professional services.

Everyone saw that my family in Hershey could not directly

handle all the inquiries and offers coming in and also care for me at the same time. The Ithaca community established a communication network. Kris and Ellen's house was at the center: questions came in, information went out. Whichever one of them was not in Pennsylvania talked to Anne or someone at the hospital and then let the local community know what was happening in Hershey.

At the hospital end, Anne was the main link in the network. Kris called regularly with a list of questions ranging from what homework from school did Satya need to how much should she tell the *Philadelphia Inquirer.* A few other close friends called the hospital, too, but acquaintances only made contact through Kris. Daily, Anne brought in stacks of messages that had come in through the pay phones on the fifth floor.

Besides channeling the efforts of acquaintances and anonymous but concerned people, Kris, Ellen, and Andrea, another friend in Ithaca, also fended off the media. The word had gone out to the community not to talk to anyone from any newspaper, magazine, television or radio station. Until the killer was caught, if ever, the police wanted as few details about the shooting known to the public as possible.

The media, on the other hand, were calling anyone they could dig up who might have any vague connection to me or Rebecca—people from our work, families, hometowns. Most of the people contacted, having gotten the message through the grapevine that it was imperative not to talk, referred the calls to Kris. Kris and Ellen's house was barraged. Miraculously, almost no information leaked out.

Through our friend Susan, Kris was able to reach Kevin Berrill, the director of the National Gay and Lesbian Task Force Anti-Violence Project. By Sunday, they had had a long discussion about antigay violence. Kevin talked about other cases, and his solid knowledge and clear perspective calmed Kris. He gave advice about the media, and recommended that I come out to the police as soon as possible.

Kevin explained that often, when cases go to trial and the truth has not been told up front, the gay victim becomes an "unreliable witness" in the jurors' minds, and the whole prosecution's case goes down the tubes. He gave an example from a case in Michigan: Gay guy goes home with someone he meets at a bar. They've been flirting all night. Then he is attacked, stabbed repeatedly. He survives, reports it to the police, but denies that his intention, and his attacker's seeming intention, was a sexual liaison. When the defense raises the issue of homosexuality, the prosecution isn't ready for it, and the victim loses all his credibility.

Even if the police and lawyers for the prosecution are going to be homophobic, Kevin advised, it's better to come out. Give the police all the information they need to solve the case. Help the prosecution be as prepared as possible to win in court, if it gets to court. He said that it was much easier to educate a D.A. ignorant of lesbian issues than it was to recover from a fall from grace in the courtroom.

Despite the fact that gay victims already have one strike against them, Kevin still recommended that we tell the police everything. This message was relayed through Kris to Anne to me, and all of us in Hershey began to discuss what to do.

At the same time, though, Kevin said that we should not let the media take over the case. A victim has a right to privacy. If the media took control—even the gay and lesbian media—I could potentially be revictimized. To a reporter trying to get my friends and family to "talk," the public "right to know" is more important than my personal privacy, my healing, or the case being solved.

By the next day, Monday, more of Susan's networking had paid off. She found Abbe Smith, a gay-positive public defender and law professor based in Philadelphia. Over the phone, Abbe assured Susan that the issue of homosexuality, at least according to Pennsylvania law, should not play into the case. In twenty-five states it is "unlawful for consenting adults to engage in sexual conduct with a member of the same sex." According to Abbe, however, Pennsylvania was not one of them.

Despite this technical acceptance of homosexuality by the state, Abbe knew that we had good reason to want a lawyer. She herself was not ready to take the case on; she thought that someone familiar with local law would be more useful. She recommended several lawyers and gave one last piece of advice: Tell the police everything. Like Kevin Berrill, her counsel was to disclose the absolute truth—exactly what had happened on May 12 and 13, that Rebecca and I had been lovers, that we were making love when the shooting occurred.

On Wednesday morning, Anne told Denny that I was ready to talk. He had been waiting for four long days, sometimes working as much as eighteen hours a day. He and Don Blevins came in, dressed as usual in sport coats and polo shirts. Denny had been around on a daily, almost hourly, basis. Don was here this morning as chief investigator in the case, which fell under the jurisdiction of the Adams County state police. Like Denny, Don had a boyish grin that let his warmth show, but he had darker hair and more of a Western Pennsylvania twang to his speech. They both settled into the chairs to the left of my bed, and Denny's gravelly voice recorded the time and place on his hand-held tape recorder. Anne was on the other side of the bed.

"I am not embarrassed at all about what I'm going to tell you," I began.

Denny and Don seemed very interested but unsurprised at this opening. I didn't wonder why too much, right then. I was concentrating on telling the story.

"Rebecca and I were lovers," I said. "I didn't tell you that at the beginning because I didn't know what the fact that I was a lesbian would mean to you. I didn't know what you would do with it. I've never been ashamed of Rebecca's and my relationship. It was wonderful, and honorable, and we loved each other."

I cried. I told them the whole story, from how long I had known Rebecca, to us deciding where to camp, to Rebecca discovering the weird guy at the campsite, to getting shot. When I got to the part about walking out of the woods, as I described each segment of my journey, Don would shake his head and blow a little stream of air from between his lips. Denny nodded silently.

When I finished, both sides of the sixty-minute tape were filled. The officers looked at me, paused, and seemed to be seeing the murder scene in their minds, now with the conspicuous gaps—particularly the one labeled *motive*—filled in. One gap remained: Who had done it?

Don had some questions for me about how our attacker had walked. When Rebecca and I had seen him walking, he hadn't been "our attacker," so I hadn't paid particular attention to anything about him. In fact, I remembered almost nothing of what he looked like, except that he was tall and thin and had been wearing grey sweatpants with a maroon stripe. I told Don I couldn't remember how he had walked. Don prompted me with some general questions about his gait, but they didn't ring any bells. Finally, he told me that he was trying to get at whether the guy had a limp.

I inhaled, leaned back, and closed my eyes. I imagined Rebecca and myself at the intersection where we were deciding which way to hike around the loop, and then hearing the mocking voice. I played out the scenario in my head, watching the unknown man walking toward us down the sloping trail, and then after the interaction, looking over my shoulder to see him walk away. I opened my eyes and told Don that the man I had seen definitely did not have a limp.

"Okay," Don said. He seemed impressed. Denny, standing and miming a hunting rifle slung over his shoulder, asked me questions about what the gun had looked like. I didn't have much to say except what I had already told them.

They thanked me and let us know how the investigation was going. We chatted a bit, and then they left. I was relieved and tired. Now we didn't have to watch what we said around anybody, and we didn't have to stop conversations in the middle when a nurse came in. Anne and I both sighed.

Evelyn and Karen visited me for the second time the same afternoon I came out to the police. Evelyn was the one member of Rebecca's family who had really gotten to know me because she and Rebecca had lived together in Blacksburg. Still, seeing her for the first time the day before had been scary. Her sister was dead. Did she blame me? Was she angry that Rebecca had died and I had lived? Did she wish that the situation had been reversed? Also, since there was a strong physical resemblance between Rebecca and Evelyn, was she going to remind me of my lover too much?

When Evelyn first arrived, my sense of devastation multiplied. My physical recovery, grief, and trauma, combined with her anguish, seemed to take the oxygen from the room. Evelyn's sister had come to meet me six days ago from the home they had shared, and now Rebecca was dead.

By the second visit, physical sensation was returning to my body. At the end of each four-hour crest of morphine the pain became fierce, and I tracked the moments on my perfectly aligned clock until the nurse came with the next dose. I begged my friends to hurry the nurse with the injections. I began to notice other, smaller things as well, like the residue of dirt and my own dried blood in the creases of my body, under my fingernails, and on my scalp.

When I mentioned how itchy and dirty my head felt, Evelyn suggested that we wash my hair. Karen helped me get out of bed and stand, bent over, near the sink in my room. Evelyn

poured cups of warm water over my head which dissolved the
dried blood matting my hair. Blood was caked around my ears.
Carefully massaging around the stitched wound at the back of
my head, her fingers gently loosened the blood clots stuck to
my scalp and the dirt that had collected. She rinsed my hair and
then brushed out the tangles. It took a long time, and we joked
about it, except that the stitch holding the tube in my nose
made it hurt to laugh.

Though Evelyn looked a lot like her sister, I didn't feel as
though I was seeing Rebecca's ghost. There were other rever-
berations in the room, though. Rebecca had come out to her siblings, but she was not out to her father or stepmother. Now, her
silence and her death seemed to amplify each other: Fear of a
homophobic response had kept her closeted. A homophobic man
had killed her. Rebecca was dead. She had never come out. We
were lesbians, we had been shot. She was dead.

Evelyn left. Karen was with me when Anne came back to
the room. Also a graduate student at Virginia Tech, Karen was
earning an advanced degree in plant biology. Unlike my friends
from Ithaca, she had known Rebecca well. The pain in the room
was sharp and full as we remembered Rebecca together.

"She's dead," I said, over and over. "Rebecca's dead, Karen."

"I know. I can't believe it. I'm so, so sorry."

Perhaps it was the loving connection with Rebecca we both
had shared that made space for the extraordinary event about to
occur, or perhaps it was the amethyst crystal.

Anne sat on the side of my bed, near me. The three of us
talked softly for a bit and cried about Rebecca. Karen held one
of my hands, and the purple crystal Anne had brought for me a
few days before rested in the other.

Suddenly, everything started looking grey behind my eyelids. I didn't know why. I could see fine a moment before.

"Something's happening," I said. "I'm seeing something."

Anne later talked about how my family at the hospital was always taking their cues from me. Whatever I needed—to cry, sleep, talk—whatever it was, that was what Anne, Kris, Gina, everyone supported me to do. So it was not unusual for Anne and Karen to follow my lead and ask what I was sensing.

I told them that everything looked grey in front of my eyes, grey and blurred. I squeezed Karen's hand, and she grasped mine back. I was a little scared. They encouraged me to let whatever was happening just happen.

"Tell us what you see," Anne said.

I described static, like a fuzzy TV screen, but the snow wasn't dots, it was thin, vertical lines. Then starts and stops to the lines appeared. They looked like an art project in which the teacher has assigned the pupils to capture something with only vertical lines and absent spaces. Anne later talked about my expression changing from fear to awe as the image behind my eyelids took shape. I described in detail every change that I saw.

"Go with it, Claude," Anne said. "You're fine."

The fuzzy lines became a face. I could see straggly long hair. Stringy facial hair. Eyes. Lips. Anne and Karen followed my narration, trying to be still and quiet and also let me know they were with me.

Then I said, "It's his face."

"It's flat. Lines," I said. I kept looking at the image before me. *That was it—that's what he looked like.*

Then it started to fade away and was gradually replaced by a big field of tall, golden pampas grass, with a wind rippling through it. I told Anne and Karen about the beautiful field. It was full of light.

After that I could see normally again. I loosened my grip on Karen's hand and on the amethyst. The rock had left an imprint in the flesh of my palm.

The vision stayed with me. The whole incident had lasted

less than five minutes. When any of us talked about it later, we would say that it was Rebecca who had drawn the face of the murderer in my mind. She had sent it to me. The next day, Anne told Denny I had recovered a memory.

Continuous hospital routines punctuated the days that followed. Surgeons visited, pleased with my progress at how quickly I was able to stand, then walk.

That was my physical progress. Emotionally, I was over-stimulated and volatile. Grief and terror and the painkillers consumed me. I spoke nonstop, and my need to control my immediate environment skyrocketed. There were moments of lightness, too, like sending Satya out for chocolate from the Hershey factory. When she returned with only one bag, I told her it was not enough, "not nearly enough," and insisted my father go for more. Later that night, nurses found piles of Hershey's miniatures on their desks.

I couldn't swallow yet, so I was being fed through a tube in my nose which had been inserted during surgery. It was a strange and extremely unpleasant feeling to have my stomach fill up while nothing had gone down my throat, to eat without eating. Although I was miserable, I joked with the nurses as they tried all the variations they could think of to make my taking in the bags of "food" more comfortable. It never was. The nurses' ease with me seemed to increase, though, as they got to know me. We wondered which was more frightening for them: the shooting or the lesbianism.

By Friday—it was May 20, exactly one week after the shooting—I was recovered enough for the Pennsylvania state police to bring a composite photo artist to my fifth floor hospital room. Much earlier—the morning following surgery—an officer with a "parts and pieces" kit had come to the intensive care unit with Denny.

A "parts and pieces" specialist puts together a face from hundreds of illustrations of noses, eyes, lips, foreheads, ears.

The witness must try to recall each feature of a perpetrator individually, and the pieces get shuffled around in a board like a puzzle. This type of procedure is much cheaper, therefore much more common, than the work of an actual composite artist, and, according to Denny, much less accurate. Denny always said that it was a crumb of investigative luck I was not well enough the first day to begin making the composite, because they might never have chosen to bring in a real artist.

I still had an IV in my arm and a tube up my nose, but a heart monitor was no longer beeping nearby. By the next day I would be wandering around the floor at three o'clock in the morning, sleepless, talking to the nurses.

In the six days between the thirteenth and the twentieth, the state police had investigated the case enough to decide to expend the extra effort, money, and time to fly in Lewis Trowbridge, an FBI-trained artist from the New Jersey state police. Denny accompanied him to the hospital. Though normal police procedure dictates that a witness be alone when she or he is questioned, we had already made it clear that my being alone, under any circumstances, was out of the question. Anne was at my side when Denny arrived. Denny introduced us to Lewis and then left.

Lew was tall and broad-shouldered, with light brown hair that fell straight over one eye. He explained the composite process thoroughly. Then he asked some basic questions about our assailant, quickly gaining my trust by poking fun at his own features, the things about his body that, on another person, would have made them self-conscious. He used his body in loose and funny ways to jog the corners of my memory about the attacker's overall appearance.

"Was he white or black?... About what age would you say he was?... And his height?... Tall...how tall? Taller than you? How about me? Oh, very tall! And thin.... Creepy, huh? Very creepy.... Kind of scruffy?... Did you notice anything about the way he walked or stood?"

He exuded an unruffled confidence in his own talents, in my ability to remember and describe what he needed, and our potential for working as a team. He told me that some things would be easy to recall, others more difficult, and that that was fine. Whether it was a gift Lew was born with, or the FBI trained their artists to be empathetic, I felt bolstered by Lew's assurances that there were no time clocks or rules about how and when I would describe things.

Plus, he sincerely valued intuition. Even if we were talking about eyes, he said, and I thought of something about lips, I should tell him. Even if I had no idea why something grabbed me, or I had a strange feeling, I should just tell him. I never let him know that the picture I was working with was mostly the one Rebecca had shown me a few days before, but the fact was he probably would not have laughed at even that.

When we were ready to move on to specifics, Lew named several possible categories with which to begin. "What do you remember best about him?"

"Hair," I said to him, and that's where we started.

From one of two hefty metal suitcases, Lew began showing me mug shots on cards sorted into stacks by facial features. It wasn't easy for me to deliberately recall the face of the man who had shot me and killed Rebecca. Sometimes I had to stop and breathe deeply or cry to calm myself. Anne would hold me or hold my hand. Lew encouraged me to take my time during the entire process. He conveyed the sense that this was the most important and serious and enjoyable thing he could be doing, which both relaxed me and gave our work together an almost magical tone. I was able to concentrate on each detail for long stretches of time.

I remembered the shaggy hair which was approximately shoulder length. Lew gave me a stack of "hair" cards and told me to separate out any that triggered a memory in me, reminding me not to be rigidly concentrating on that category, to pull any card that moved me for any reason.

It took hours. Each facial feature had its own set of cards, and with the same concentration with which we had begun the last stack, we would pore through the next. Hair, nose, shape of face, mouth, eyes, lips. Lew knew every one, all the noses, all the chins. Sometimes he would pull out a few cards to show me, from my description or if a certain combination made sense to him. Then he might take a number that I had chosen and say, "All of these noses have nostrils that turn upward, and these others are set particularly low on the face. Which did you mean?" Sometimes I was able to articulate what I meant and sometimes I just chose. Sometimes talking about it further would clarify a choice, but if I didn't know, Lew seemed content to leave the "why" of my choice unexamined.

While going through the last set of cards, one particular mug shot spooked me so much that I wanted to keep it face down on my bed. My body shook when I looked at it, although I could not say why. The eyes of the person in the photograph were extraordinarily deep-set. We figured out later that it must have been those sunken eyes that made me shudder. They were a facial detail of the murderer I could not have consciously re-membered, but which something deep in me recognized.

There were very few interruptions. Once a nurse came in with codeine for me. Lew began to make sense of my narrowing assortment of facial features, and finally, when we had finished all the categories, I took a break and Lew started to sketch. He sat with the cards in front of him and drew quietly for twenty minutes. Anne and I spoke softly to each other. There was al-most a sense of sacredness to the process: The composite was the most important contribution I could make toward captur-ing the man who killed Rebecca.

My vision on Wednesday had been only brief and incom-plete, and throughout the entire assembling of the composite, I never wholly reimagined our assailant's face. When Lew finished the pencil sketch, I did not want to see it. He had shown it to Anne a few times as he worked, to whom it meant nothing. My body was rigid; Anne held me as Lew flipped his pad around. I shrank back from the drawing. He and Anne knew from my reaction that the drawing was good.

When I was ready, Lew questioned me about what was right, what was wrong. I looked away, looked back, looked away again, correcting one feature at a time. "He looks too young." I turned my head, turned back. "He doesn't look straggly enough." I barely glanced at the sketch. "The mouth is wrong." Lew erased portions, redrew them, erased again.

Changing one feature, Lew explained, would influence the make-up of the entire face. The nose could not become longer without affecting the mouth and eyes and cheek structures. My admiration for him grew with each rendition of the composite.

Finally, after many revisions, he said, "On a scale of one to ten, how much does this feel like the individual you saw on the trail?" My response was 75 to 85 percent. Lew was satisfied, knowing from experience that 100 percent was unattainable. He told me that people looked different enough from each other that 75 percent correct was more than enough to recognize someone.

Over three hours had passed. Gina and my parents were at the hospital that day, waiting in the lounge. Denny had waited, too, pacing the lounge like an expectant father. He later said he wanted to come in many times and see how it was going, but knew he shouldn't interrupt the process. Finally, Lew called him in.

"Did you get something?" he asked Lew, and to me, "You must be exhausted." We both nodded.

Lew bid us farewell, and Denny left to take him to the airport. Anne and I remained together in the room, looking around, refocusing on the day, the time. Everything had faded except for shapes of faces and subtleties of features. Anne got up and shook out her limbs. I stretched in my bed.

➤

Denny had been a police officer all of his adult life. He had almost enough time with the force to begin to collect a pension, although he was only in his forties. His wife worried about him often, now more than usual. Denny had spent little time with her or their children in Harrisburg since last week, and he was barely sleeping. His assignment on this case had been pure luck: He had been on-call the Friday of the shooting and had gone to the hospital as backup to a rookie.

Denny strode into police headquarters late Friday afternoon, holding the composite in his hand. He had seen Lew Trowbridge off, then gone directly to where the team of investigators was still at work. He threw the composite on a desk where eight or ten photographs also lay, face-down. Several officers were nearby. When one saw the drawing, he reached for a photo in the nearby pile and turned it over. They matched like cards in a game of Concentration. "We've got our man," Denny said.

Undercover police officers had interviewed approximately two hundred people at private homes, in bars, and in town. A $500 reward had been issued for any information leading to the arrest of the murderer, and someone had called with an anonymous tip suggesting Stephen Roy Carr just a few days before. He became one of five suspects. Carr was a wanderer who lived in the woods, staying occasionally with the few acquaintances he had locally. He was likely to have been in the area of the shooting. He had served time in a Florida prison. He was known to hunt. Until now, he had not been a strong suspect.

It had only been two days since Denny and Don had decided that they could fully trust Claudia. The first day of the investigation, the police had thoroughly searched both Claudia's and Rebecca's backpacks and cars. A book of lesbian erotica, pink triangle bumper stickers, and other bits and pieces of their lives were strewn in side pockets and back seats. It would have been hard for them to miss that the two women were lesbians, and it was a good guess that they were lovers. No one, however, would tell Denny that directly, until Wednesday, even under pressure and leading questions. So he and Don had been suspicious, knowing there was a large part of the story Claudia wasn't revealing.

The only contact Denny had had before with lesbians was a jealous stabbing between one half of a couple and "the other woman." When the shooting happened, and all indications were that the victims were lesbians, the jealousy motive was the first thing he thought of. He had also guessed Anne's relationship to Claudia and had considered her a suspect for several days.

Higher-ups had put a lot of pressure on Denny to question Claudia more rigorously. *Put more pressure on her. Get her to crack.* He and Don had had to fend them off, believing they were more likely to get what they wanted if Claudia felt safe. They didn't want her to bolt.

With such a large part of the story so obviously missing, they were forced to be patient. It helped that Denny and Don had an enormous amount of work to do. After Claudia told them directly about her sexual orientation, and shared her conviction that she and Rebecca had been shot because they were lesbians, the motive was clear. It was certainly the most likely explanation. Anne was, at least for Denny and Don, removed from the list of suspects. Denny had actually stopped thinking of Anne as a suspect days earlier, once he got to know her and saw her connection with Claudia. Now with the composite, they not only had a motive, they had a murderer.

The composite was one of the last links in a chain of circumstances allying the Pennsylvania state police with me and my community. The other links were a combination of honesty, excellent police work, a horrifying crime and criminal, luck, strength, and race and class status.

Too often the law is in cahoots with the perpetrators of bias-related crimes. In the infamous "Greensboro Massacre," for example, five anti-Klan demonstrators were killed. When the police arrived, they began arresting the surviving demonstrators, not the KKK members with guns. When the case came to trial, all six of the Nazis and Klansmen accused of murder were found not guilty.

Sometimes the discrimination is more subtle: Law enforcement does not use all of its resources to try to solve the crime or mitigate the pain of the survivor or the victim's family. The police system frequently treats lesbian and gay victims of crimes in this way. The message is: You were asking for it by being too "out," or, your lifestyle is abnormal, disgusting, and sinful anyway.

The individual officers on this case, however—Denny Beaver and Don Blevins—became bonded with me. Although they were no less homophobic than the average state trooper, their units no more enlightened, they became committed to me, a lesbian crime victim, and my lesbian family. Denny and Don eventually spoke of how they were needled about the case, and how, No, they still wouldn't really want their son or daughter to be gay, but they were solidly on my side.

The bonding probably began the night of the shooting. The story I related to the police was accurate and clear, and they were very quickly able to verify it: I told them precisely where we had been on the trail. They found the scene as I had described it. Their own police work recovered significant physical evidence. So, right from the beginning, Denny and Don were able to regard me as extremely credible, and as a witness my credibility was crucial to the prosecution.

As the investigation went on, the police not only continued to believe in my memory of the facts, but their hearts also softened. Rebecca and I were clearly innocent; we were two unarmed women on a camping trip. There was no grey area in this crime, no complex interpersonal issues or mitigating prior relationships. Stephen Roy Carr was a complete stranger. He had murdered Rebecca and had tried to murder me. Moreover, Denny had seen my desperate condition that first night in the trauma unit.

The brutality of the murder was out of the ordinary for rural Adams County, where there was an average of four murders a year, usually involving people known to each other. The local community was shocked and outraged. The Appalachian Trail was almost sacrosanct to native residents: An atrocity there was akin to one in a schoolyard or a playground. It was a place where locals would take their Boy Scout troops and sixth-grade classes for an overnight. Besides, no one wanted an unsolved murder to detract from the tourism the Appalachian Trail brought to the area.

Both the police and local community were impressed with my strength. The police, in particular, respected my physical stamina, having retraced my four-mile hike—without taking five bullet wounds first. The police also saw the campsite, with the tarp covered in blood and crumpled with signs of Rebecca's and my frantic movements. The officers understood that I had been shot, had seen my lover murdered, and then saved myself. I credited this "machismo" to survival instincts, but it contributed to making the police, as Abbe said later, "founding members of the Claudia Brenner Fan Club."

All of these factors—especially when contrasted with Stephen Roy Carr's cold-bloodedness—predisposed the police to like me. Plus, the case was going well.

The fact that my chosen family were all white, mostly middle-class, educated women also had a positive effect on the attitude of the authorities. As did my white, middle-class, educated, married parents coming to support me. The people around me mostly fit into categories that were not threatening to the police. It was easy to see them as "respectable citizens."

My coming out, far from being a surprise to Denny and Don, had actually eliminated any lingering suspicions that I was not telling the complete truth. Virtually positive from the first day that I was a lesbian, they came to see me as an honest, strong, sociable woman. I was a real person, the survivor of a violent crime. And the women whom the police dealt with every day at the hospital in Hershey, who cared for me in a way that few families or communities can muster, these women who were lesbians did not fit Denny or Don's stereotypes of "dykes" either. So when Lew and I finished the composite, it was the final element in the fortuitous mix solidifying my—and my community's—bond with the Pennsylvania state police.

                      ➤

Several hours had passed since we finished the composite. We did not expect Denny back that night. Anne was taking a break, and my mother and Gina were with me, my mother in a chair to my left, Gina on the end of the bed. My mother and father had been back and forth to Hershey several times that week. Even though my chosen family and community were a bit foreign to them, my parents were supportive of me and seemed comfortable with everyone at the hospital.

The head of my bed was cranked up, so I was almost sitting, and I could see out the windows on the wall behind my mother. It was dark outside. The three of us were looking at the map of Michaux State Forest that Denny had brought us earlier. It was identical to the one Rebecca and I had used, the one with the blood on it that I had given to the state police.

Rebecca had been dead for a week, almost to the hour. I was recreating every segment of our journey a week earlier. "Right now, we were just setting up camp." "Now, a week ago, I was still walking along the state forest road. That Blazer had probably passed me already." We were looking at the map, tracing my movements. It was then that we noticed the name of the road on which Rebecca and I had parked: Dead Woman's Hollow Road.

Suddenly, Denny burst into the room, bags showing under his eyes, but exhilarated. The composite was a gold mine, he told us. From the five suspects under investigation, the police were able to immmediately eliminate four and focus on the fifth, the man who matched the composite. Denny swept the four innocent men away with the movement of his arm across an imaginary desk.

Denny wanted me, now, to attempt to identify the murderer. But, he told us, the only photo available was one that had been taken ten years earlier.

Now? Already? What if I couldn't pick him out, or picked the wrong one? An ID seemed so official. I was scared, too, that the photos would make him more real, make the murder more real, make Rebecca more dead. The work of the composite had only been finished hours before, and I was exhausted, but I could not say no.

Denny took out his small tape recorder and identified the time, place, people present, and described the identification procedure about to take place. I asked my mother if she wanted to stay for this part. She did, and so did Gina.

Denny placed five photos before me on the bed. I looked. And looked. Gina looked with me but, of course, she had no idea who Stephen Roy Carr was. None of the people in the pictures looked enough like the man I had seen for me to be definitive. More than anything, I didn't want to identify him wrongly. After a bit, I told Denny I didn't know. There was a photo that grabbed me, but I didn't know. It turned out that that photo was not of Carr. I was disappointed not to have been able to pick the right photograph, but the one of Stephen Roy Carr was ten years old, a snapshot taken at a party where he was dressed in a costume. Denny told me it didn't matter that much; they were very confident they knew who the murderer was. Now they just needed to find him.

,

As the police conducted the manhunt for Rebecca's murderer, I was getting ready to leave the hospital. The IV in my arm and the tube in my nose finally came out on Saturday. Hospital staff brought me food, but I couldn't swallow it. It was hard enough getting down the liquid codeine I needed every four hours. Satya sat with me the first time I managed it, using the technique the hospital had taught me my first night in the x-ray room. *One, two, three, try not to clench, swallow!* I held her hand, squeezing hard as I swallowed each small sip.

My mother couldn't hide her disappointment at my failed efforts to eat and our fruitless search for something nourishing that would slide down less painfully. Another day went by and I had the irrational idea I would starve to death there, at a university medical center. When my mother thought of baby food, she was thrilled. She and my dad went out immediately and bought some. I ate it gratefully. I had had nothing enter my stomach via my mouth for eight days. Gourmet horizons of creamed spinach and strained carrots opened up. Mashed tofu was to become a staple at home.

There were many details to take care of before I was released from Hershey Medical Center on Monday May 23. The medical social worker sought me out to discuss bills and possible payment options, including the Pennsylvania Crime Victims Compensation Fund and Medicaid. She let me know that the fees the surgeons charged me were extraordinarily low. They have that kind of flexibility with fees at a teaching hospital, she explained. She went on to tell me that the doctors were salaried and the clinic just needed to meet expenses. They knew I didn't have insurance.

I had an exit exam at the ear, nose, and throat outpatient

clinic. As I waited in the hall, I sat near a person with a computerized voice. Only then did I understand the good fortune of having my vocal chords intact. I bought codeine, antibiotics, and sleeping pills at the hospital pharmacy. The E.M.T. from Life Lion flight service accompanied me to the hangar to see the helicopter in which I had flown eleven days before, and with her I was able to reconstruct the terrifying journey I had taken.

Finally, good-byes exchanged with the hospital staff, belongings gathered from where they had spread over the fifth floor, helicopter T-shirt purchased, we finally left the hospital complex. Anne and Gina had become acquainted with the town of Hershey in their ten days there, and we stopped at a grocery store in a nearby shopping center. I stayed in the backseat of the car while they went into the store, dazed that I was seeing an unfamiliar town, one I had entered by air, by night, and in shock. I was scared in my few moments alone. I was certain that if I went into the store, or anywhere in public, everyone would know who I was.

Anne and Gina returned, and I spent the five hour trip going home to Ithaca lying in the backseat of the big, borrowed car, getting used to my new layers of pain.

ꞋFOURꞋ

On Monday, May 23, fourteen horses, five teams of dogs, and squads of trained officers were flown in from the Maryland state police. Maryland also provided two search helicopters. Don Blevins set up a command post in the center of Pine Grove Furnace State Park, on the top of Big Flat Mountain, in order to keep track of all the activity.

Don and Denny and the rest of the team of police officers did a lot of detective work in the three days between the time the composite was drawn and the day of the manhunt. They discovered that in the past, Stephen Roy Carr had sometimes stayed in Shippensburg with a family named Gulden, and had hunted birds in the woods behind their house with their teenage son. When questioned, the family reported that on Friday night, May 13, Carr came to their home. The next morning he told the seventeen-year-old boy that he had done a terrible thing, but he never said what. He left later that day.

The investigators searched for spent casings where Carr and the Gulden son had hunted birds, and the ones they found matched the casings the original team had located in the woods near the Rocky Knob Trail. The family also had a white cat, and forensics concluded that the white hairs stuck to the knitted cap, which had been left near the unused ammunition, were from the same animal. All of this made clear to Don that the person wearing the hat, the owner of the murder weapon, and the man who had occasionally visited the Guldens were undoubtedly the same person: Stephen Roy Carr.

Carr had an uncle who lived in Cleversburg, a few miles away, and the uncle had allowed Carr to build a sort of cave on his property where his nephew kept a few things and stayed from time to time. The uncle gave the police some belongings of Carr's from the cave—a towel, a shirt—and from these items the bloodhounds were able to pick up Carr's scent in the forest that morning.

The officers radioing back to Don throughout the day said the dogs were tearing up the woods in all directions, teams of police running in tow. Stephen Roy Carr's scent must have been everywhere. The dogs uncovered many places where Carr seemed to have slept or stopped, some of them lean-tos, some of them just holes in the ground covered by sticks and branches. But each trail eventually ended, and the dogs would circle around the area, noses to the ground, whining. The helicopters and the mounted officers, including Denny—who had not ridden a horse in twenty years—also scoured the area for any signs of Carr's route, but they all came up empty.

That night, the police decided they would release the composite to the media. If Carr was paying any attention to the news, he would already know that Claudia had survived. If his composite was circulated and he realized that he was wanted before someone else recognized him and told the police of his whereabouts, there was a good chance he would try to make himself disappear. The investigators had no idea what kind of resources he had for travel. He might hook up with someone, or hitchhike, and be five hundred miles away in a day. But they had reached a dead end following the leads they already had, so they decided to take their chances.

⸻

Late Monday afternoon, we arrived without incident at Anne's wood-frame duplex on the corner of Wood Street in Ithaca. I found the worn furniture inside and the walls that needed painting familiar and welcoming.

Ruth, Anne's housemate, had generously offered to share her room with me. Even had there been a spare space in the house, I wanted to share a room; I still needed people with me, especially at night. I vividly remembered the massive nightmare I had had in the hospital, awakening the fifth floor with screams that sent nurses flying to my room:

Blackness. So black you can't distinguish its blackness. An utter void with no boundaries. The only force is pulling downward. It is a powerful force. My being wants to go upward. The force wants me to go downward. The force is much more powerful than I am. I am a clump of dust. It is an immense vortex. There are no edges to grab hold of. No places to push off with my arms to stabilize myself. Just blackness pulling me in. I am resisting the blackness with all the strength in every fiber of my body. I move neither down nor up. I start to scream. The blackness is still all around me but my eyes are open. I am screaming and screaming and screaming.

I flailed myself upright, propelled to the end of the bed. The IV tube connected to my hand was strained to its limit, my knees pressing against the cold metal of the hospital bed rail. Screaming. Gina and then Anne bolted alert, the passage between dozing and consciousness almost instantaneous. I didn't see them or hear their reassuring words. Screaming.

Footsteps like galloping horses in the hall. The first nurse to arrive came in the door. The white uniform. She rushed to the bed and hugged me. I clung to her for long minutes. Her large breasts were comforting.

For the remainder of the night, I sat leaning against Anne in the bed, her arms around me. There was no suggestion of sleep, no words. We just waited for the light of morning.

Now it had to be my own household that appeared at my bedside, and more than once in the succeeding weeks, it was Gina who appeared when the noise I made in my sleep sounded like the murder was happening all over again. Gina would run in saying, "It's okay, it's okay, it's Gina, it's okay, you're safe," before Anne was even out from under her covers. Gina's steadying presence brought us closer together, stretching us toward friendship and away from the competitiveness between "ex-lover" and "new lover."

I began sitting *shiva** for Rebecca two days after I returned to Ithaca. I was raised religiously observant—my family went to synagogue almost every week. But ever since leaving my parents' home I had been a cultural Jew, celebrating Shabbat and Passover at home but never going to organized services. In coping with Rebecca's death, however, I turned to Judaism for guidance. My parents supported my choice to mourn Rebecca in a traditional way, even though she was not a Jew. The letter of Jewish law says that one sits *shiva* for immediate family: parents, siblings, children, or a spouse. In the spirit of Jewish law, Karen and I would mourn our friend and my lover together. My mother was the one who brought me the *yahrzeit* memorial candle which I lit on that first of seven days of mourning.

Sunday, May 22, was an incredible spring day. The grassy clearing near Blacksburg, Virginia where people gathered was brightly sunlit, and the tall trees surrounding it created deep shadows. The ground was covered in grasses and wildflowers and may apples. There were mountains in the distance and the sound of a nearby waterfall.

Evelyn and Rebecca's closest friends had planned this memorial service, deliberately choosing a beautiful, outdoor place

*The Jewish observance following the death of a loved one.

both to honor Rebecca's love of nature and to reclaim the out-doors after her murder. The clearing seemed to grow to the per-fect size for the huge circle of over 150 people who had come to celebrate her life.

Evelyn burned sage that she and Rebecca had grown in their garden. Rebecca's friends brought rituals from diverse faiths. There was singing, dancing, and poetry. All mourned the loss of the warm, personal relationships Rebecca had established with them. To one close friend, Chris, it seemed that Rebecca's spirit was hovering over the circle at the height of the trees. Everyone who wanted had an opportunity to step into the circle and say something they had learned from or enjoyed about Rebecca. The shared eulogy went on for a long time.

Traditional Mennonites don't watch television or read the papers, so although the case was all over the news, the Weavers apparently had no suspicions that they were harboring a mur-derer. It had been nearly a week since the shooting. When the composite was released on Monday, May 23, a Mennonite slightly less pious than the Weavers saw the drawing of Stephen Roy Carr's face in the newspaper or on TV, and recognized him as the stranger who had been in church with the Weavers the previous Sunday. That "sinner" informed the church preacher of Carr's identity, and on Tuesday morning, May 24, the police received a phone call from the Mennonite minister.

Instantly, the state police began organizing for the capture. It took several hours to call in the two dozen police officers needed to roadblock the Weavers' farm. More officers, includ-ing a S.W.A.T. team in full camouflage gear, went to surround the farmyard itself. Mr. and Mrs. Weaver were informed that the man who was staying with them, who was now out in the fields with their son, was wanted for murder.

Denny was miles away at this point, sore from the previous day on horseback, manning a roadblock. He yearned to be the one to arrest Stephen Roy Carr himself, but as Carr was considered "armed and dangerous," a S.W.A.T. officer had to do it.

After leaving the Guldens' home on Saturday May 14, Stephen Roy Carr had traveled north out of Shippensburg until he reached a small creek, the Conodoguinet. He found a shallow metal tub meant for mixing cement mortar, climbed in, and floated downstream for two days. After going about five miles from Shippensburg, as the crow flies, he climbed out of the creek in Cumberland County, "Amish country."

He made up a name and a hard-luck story for the Mennonite woman who helped him to shore, and asked if he could stay with them and work for some meals for a little while. The woman whose farm property he was on, named Weaver, agreed to take him in. The family gave him a pair of boots which he said he would work off, fed him, and let him sleep in their barn.

At the roadblock, Denny and several other officers were stopping the few cars that approached and redirecting them around the scene. One car pulled up with a young man in the driver's seat. Denny asked where he was going. "That's my farm up there," the man said.

"Do you know the Weavers?" Denny asked.

"They're my parents," the man said.

Denny explained the situation. When the oldest Weaver son heard that the man at his parents' was wanted for murder, he told Denny that at that very moment, Carr was on his way over to his own farm, which bordered his parents', transporting a truckload of heifers with his younger brother.

The S.W.A.T. police team at the elder Weavers' farm were going to miss Carr entirely. Denny and two other state troopers, Officer Donelly and Corporal O'Brien, jumped into a car and followed the Weavers' son to his farm, radioing the change in circumstance to the commanding officer at the Weavers'. The Weavers' son estimated that Carr and his brother were going to arrive in his farmyard in about fifteen minutes.

The yard was bordered by several buildings surrounding a half-circle driveway. A fence enclosing a cow pasture ran in a straight line in back of the entire farmyard and driveway area. After concealing the police car, Donelly hid behind the farmhouse itself, which was to the left of the drive. O'Brien was to the right, in the garage. Denny situated himself inside the milkhouse, which was at the top curve of the drive in front of the wooden fence, and held his twelve-gauge shotgun ready.

Moments before Carr and the younger Weaver son were to appear, another vehicle pulled up, driven by two members of the S.W.A.T. team. The car was hastily parked behind a building, and then the two khaki-clad occupants burst out and ran for cover, toward the same garage as Corporal O'Brien. They crawled under the cracked-open garage door, both wearing full backpacks. One got his pack caught on the door of the garage and was pinned between it and the floor. Denny wasn't sure how long he stopped breathing as he watched the pack being maneuvered. It came loose and the officer pulled himself into position just as the truck, its open bed loaded with cows, pulled in.

The farm truck parked at the top of the driveway in front of the milkhouse, and Stephen Roy Carr and a young man jumped out of the cab. The older Weaver sibling stood in front of the farmhouse, behind his parked car. He casually called to his brother, who walked toward him, away from the truck.

Carr headed toward the fence surrounding the pasture. No one moved. The gate was in between the farmhouse where Donelly was in back and the milkhouse where Denny hid. Carr passed the point where Donelly could have easily stopped him. If he got to the fence, and then found out that there were five guns behind him, he might decide to run. With a potential escape on their hands, someone could decide to shoot first, accuse later. Denny didn't want that to happen. He didn't want anyone to have to aim at a moving target, either.

Denny stepped out of the milkhouse when Stephen Roy
Carr was just a few yards in front of him, leveled his shotgun at
Carr's chest, and said, "You move and you're dead."

Carr froze, put his hands up, and fell to his knees. Denny
called this "brainlock": All Carr could see was the barrel of a
gun. Denny kept the rifle trained on him while Donelly came
out and put cuffs on Carr's hands and informed him that he was
under arrest. By this time, the rest of the officers who had been
stationed at the Weaver farm arrived. TV and newspaper reporters were not far behind.

⸜

Don was typing an affidavit in the D.A.'s office in Gettysburg
when the call came that Carr had been arrested. He left immediately and was brought up to date when he reached the state
police barracks in Carlisle. Carr had been properly read his
Miranda rights and had waived his right to a lawyer. Troopers
Matt O'Brien and John Holtz, both seasoned interrogators, were
questioning him.

Carr was booked under an earlier "fugitive from the state
of Florida" warrant because there was concern that they did not
yet have enough evidence against him for Rebecca's murder.
Although Don personally had no doubts about Carr's guilt, it
seemed a wise decision at the time. They could prove he was a
fugitive, and it was likely that he would give incriminating evidence about the murder in the course of the interrogation. This
was standard police procedure: Don't compromise the suspect's
rights, but don't tell them any more than they need to know.

What had he been doing since leaving Florida? Carr said
that he lived in the woods and survived by trapping, fishing,
and hunting with a gun. When they asked where his gun was,
Carr claimed it had been stolen. He even drew a picture of his
lost .22.

He explained that when he woke up in the middle of the

afternoon on Friday the thirteenth, his gun and several other things were missing. He had been sleeping on the Appalachian Trail. Officer Holtz asked if he had seen anyone else on the A.T. that day. Yes, he had seen "two girls" that morning at a campsite where he had been sleeping in a shelter. One of them talked with him for a few minutes while she was "buck naked." A little while later, they got dressed and left. "And," said Carr, "I never saw them again."

"We have some good news for you," Trooper Holtz said to Carr. "We recovered some of your stolen property. It was found at the scene of a murder."

Carr began to cry. "Why does this always happen to me?" he said. "I left the trail. I slept at my aunt's all day. My gun was stolen."

Holtz and O'Brien told Carr they knew he had been to the Gulden family's house on the fourteenth, and that he had talked about doing a terrible thing. Carr denied everything, saying he had first heard of the shooting on the six o'clock news. He was asked again whether he had seen "the girls" after the morning of the thirteenth. When he replied "No," Trooper Holtz looked directly at Carr and said, "One of them lived."

Stephen Roy Carr cried even louder. "If I tell you the truth," he said, "you'll put me away for a long time. I should have run."

He was asked if perhaps the shooting could have been an accident. A few minutes later he said that, yes, it was an accident. He saw movement, he thought it was a deer, he shot. After five or more shots, he said, he heard screaming, and he picked up his gear and ran. Buried the gun. Would you show us where you hid it? Trooper Holtz asked. Carr said that he would.

Officers Holtz, O'Brien, and Blevins brought Carr back to Shippensburg Road, followed by a cavalcade of media and a few other police. While in transport to the weapon, John Holtz bantered with Carr. "Now tell me the truth," the trooper asked, "did you really see them kissing?" Carr had mentioned earlier that he had seen "the girls" kissing. He had also talked distastefully of the Mennonites because he didn't like the fact that the men kissed the men and the women kissed the women. Carr laughed and said that they were doing a lot more than that. After he settled himself in the brush on Friday afternoon, Carr said, he saw "the girls eating each other out."

When they arrived at the curve of the road near where Carr had hidden the weapon, he had no trouble pointing out the exact anonymous-looking steep embankment where his .22 was buried. It happened to be less than a mile from the place where Claudia had been picked up by the two boys the night of the shooting. The rifle was under a tree stump, Carr told John Holtz, describing which one. He had wrapped plastic around his prized possession so it would stay dry.

The forensics lab later determined that the retrieved gun precisely matched the ballistic markings on eight spent casings found near the Rocky Knob Trail, as well as the casings found at the Guldens' house. The lab also proved it was the same gun that created the markings on the one unshattered bullet that was recovered, the one that had entered Rebecca's back, pierced her liver, and lodged intact under the surface of her skin above her rib cage.

Immediately upon Carr's return to the state police barracks, a judge came to the jail and Carr was formally charged with murder.

⸙

Next to the long-burning candle in a clear glass were photographs of Rebecca and flowers. Flowers all over the house. There were no hard wooden stools and people in black clothing like in my memories of the living rooms of my youth when someone had died. But the mirrors were shrouded in cloth, and it was me and Karen tearing our clothes according to the ritual of *keriah*. Anne and Gina ripped a piece of an old dark shirt of

Anne's and symbolically wore the strip pinned to their clothing for the rest of the week.

Denny called late Tuesday while we were finishing preparations for *shiva*. I sat on the straight-backed wooden chair next to the black phone table, holding the phone half-away from my ear so that Gina, sitting across from me on the arm of the couch, could also hear Denny's telling of the story of Carr's capture and arrest. Other people were in the living room, too, and they waited expectantly to hear the news.

Denny was elated. Carr had been captured, and Denny had been the one to apprehend him. It was a big case in Adams County, Pennsylvania, and "our team" had fit the pieces together.

The police had been able to solve the case in just eleven days because everyone working on it, from Denny and Don, to the major in charge of the case in Harrisburg, had decided that the situation was a priority. They spent a lot of money and person-power, and, fortunately, the expenditures yielded early results. The inquiry did not have to continue past the point where it began to suffer from monetary pressures to cut back.

Denny was proud. Everything had gone right so far with the case, by intention or by luck, except that Rebecca was dead. When Gina and I told the others in the room that Carr was in custody, they were relieved and almost felt like celebrating. I was relieved, too, though at the time, because of my grief, all news felt like it was either bad or nothing. I was grateful, but I wasn't happy.

⸱

The structure of *shiva*, with its custom of visiting the aggrieved, helped my community in Ithaca to express their sorrow and made renewed contact with me less awkward. Many people came offering love or concern. The house was constantly full of friends. Some were able to meet me in the terror. Others brought flowers and food and condolences but couldn't stay where it was so emotionally raw.

One night, a friend who was a doctor spoke to me about death and dying. I asked him about corpses, trying to figure out whether Rebecca had died before or after I left her. He answered my questions about the likely effect the bullet had when it hit her liver. Another physician later told me exactly what the surgeons had done during the operation on my neck, how they had stretched the flesh back to access the wound and sewed the hole shut. I was fascinated by the details. They were all I had.

Jill was another acquaintance who visited during *shiva*. I knew her through the co-counseling community, but we had never been close. When she spoke to me, she offered undiluted commiseration and support, and said that if I ever wanted to counsel with her, to call. She had suffered a very severe asthma attack a few months before which had nearly been fatal, and that experience helped her approach my near-death and pain without fear. I told her thanks, that I would call soon. I did, in fact, a few days later, and began what would turn into years of counseling with her, sometimes every day.

For the Saturday evening near the end of *shiva*, the Cornell University Hillel rabbi helped me organize a *havdalah* service, the ceremony marking the close of every Shabbat. Holding a braided candle, a spice box full of cinnamon and cloves, and a cup of red wine, we blessed the Creator for distinguishing between light and dark, rest and work, the sacred and the everyday. Then we said *kaddish* for Rebecca. I had known those mourner's words most of my life, hearing them punctuate every synagogue service. I remembered the suited men standing, praying, and me, even at my young age, knowing that they had lost someone close to them. Growing up, I had thought little of what the Hebrew call and responses literally meant, but I understood that they were about death.

I made sure that when I said *kaddish* for Rebecca there were many people who could say the prayer, who had also been small and watched adults they knew stand before God and the community to mourn. At that juncture I did not have the patience or stamina to be the sole Jew amongst non-Jewish allies. I wanted the prayer like I remembered it. Between myself and my friends, the words marched from our lips in a familiar, measured memorial procession: *Yitgadal v'yitkadash sh'mai rabah....* When we were finished, everyone at the service responded with *Amen.*

Shiva literally means *seven,* but life did not really stop during those seven days of mourning. My mind and body made that impossible. Though I was still taking codeine, it did little to mask the pain I was feeling when I ate. It was not my throat that hurt so much anymore, but my teeth. I couldn't even chew pureed vegetables and mashed tofu.

I knew from the surgeons at Hershey that I had a shattered molar. However, when the oral surgeon removed the tooth, it didn't seem to help. I went to see a dentist who discovered that the adjacent tooth was badly cracked as well. At that point, the news that I might lose another tooth was more than I could bear. Loosing Rebecca was more than I could bear. The murder was more than I could bear. Having bullets and scalpels and tubes forced in and pulled out of me was more than I could bear. I felt myself capsize at the suggestion of another loss. My dentist was sensitive to this. He agreed to try and save the tooth. "We'll do our best," he said, warning me that his attempts might fail. But even his willingness to experiment mitigated one more small crisis amongst the giant crises.

I was also hardly sleeping. Far from having nightmares, I rarely even approached the deep sleep where dreams occur. Instead, frightening images appeared on my eyelids every night as I dozed off, and I would jerk myself awake, over and over again. When I was alert, the flashes faded away. The technical name for these pre-slumber visions is "hypnogogic hallucination." At the beginning stages of sleep, people have passing visions of their day or their thoughts. So, unwillingly, did I.

I was seeing a professional therapist, who donated her twice-weekly sessions with me. She told me that not sleeping made perfect sense. Who would want to become as vulnerable as we are in sleep when someone had tried to murder her? In fact, she told me, disruptive symptoms are more of a concern when they are absent in a survivor. That comforted me intellectually, but my body and emotions still felt haywire and raw.

I hated the prescribed sleeping pills and the cotton-headed feeling I woke with after their induced unconsciousness. I also dreaded awakening in the middle of the night and coping again with sleeplessness. Pills or no, I got up much too early each day. I tried to normalize sleeping by making a rule that I couldn't get out of bed until the first light. Anne and her household found the house obsessively tidy, the dishdrain full by the time the sun came up.

Company helped calm my mania. A friend provided comfort, orientation to the present, and safety. At first it was Anne or Gina who always stayed with me, fitting work and school, respectively, in between. Eventually other friends were organized to help out, both days and nights scheduled so that I was never alone.

The twenty-four-hour care had been going on for weeks. One time, in the hospital, Anne stood for so many hours that her ankles swelled to twice their size. My caregivers typically slept in two- or three-hour chunks; even when I slept, the slightest noise from me brought them instantly awake, hearts racing. Yet everyone caring for me was feeling many of the same emotions I did: shock, fatigue, sapping fear.

Karen later told me how difficult this was. Though she was committed, she felt relieved when it wasn't her night. Karen was one of the few people around me who had really known Rebecca. When she was with me at night, we mostly stared, unseeing, out between the slats of the window blinds, going over and over the reality that Rebecca was dead.

,

When Stephen Roy Carr was arrested, and we knew the case would be prosecuted, it seemed clearer than ever that I needed someone with legal expertise to look out for my interests from a feminist and gay-positive perspective. It was only after the fact that we realized I also needed someone who could advocate for "victim's rights." My extended family took up the search for a laywer again.

Abbe Smith was recontacted. There had been conversations with a few other attorneys that she had recommended, but none of them proved the right combination of feminist and competent. Susan, the lawyer friend who had originally located Abbe, called her back, and Abbe finally agreed to meet with me.

As a public defender, Abbe was usually firmly on the side of the defendant. She had also worked, however, on behalf of crime victims in domestic violence, rape, and sexual abuse cases. Most important as far as I was concerned, her advice to us had been excellent: She had advised us to tell the truth to the police.

When Susan first spoke to Abbe while I was in the hospital, her reticence about working with me was not simply that she was unfamiliar with local legal praxis and the cast of characters, but also because she was skeptical about the whole idea of separate victim representation. She didn't want to simply "hold the family's hand and appear at press conferences."

But Abbe recognized the other side of this argument:

> I had to admit that, if ever there were a case that called out for additional, independent, private counsel for a victim, this was it. Who knew what the prosecutor might be like? Who knew what political pressure might influence the handling of the case in central Pennsylvania, hardly a bedrock of social liberalism?

Who knew what evidentiary issues might arise? Who knew what the jury pool was like, and what strategies might be devised by the defense to play upon a jury's homophobia and misogyny? *

Abbe agreed to meet with me in Philadelphia on June 7. Ruth offered to drive me down, and Nancie let us convene at her house.

A map of Michaux State Forest, legal pads, and pens covered Nancie's glass coffee table as I told Abbe about the shooting. She asked lots of questions, listened well, and took notes. She also told us about her beliefs, particularly concerning the death penalty.

Abbe was against the death penalty in principle, she said, and I needed to know that since this was a capital case. It was bizarre to hear her "warning" me about her opposition to the death penalty because, in general, I had held the same views. In good liberal tradition, I—and everybody on "our side"—usually took the defendant's position, seeing the system as being harsh on defendants. And in many cases, that was true.

But it was the exact opposite in this case: We wanted to lock him up and throw away the key. Some of us wanted him dead. Despite this, Abbe's firm opinions made me more comfortable with her. I agreed with her politically, but it wasn't yet clear what stance I would take given my own experience.

We decided that Abbe would assist me, and she drew up a retainer. She would provide advice, serve as a liaison with the court system and D.A.'s office, and try to translate our concerns into the terminology of the court.

Ruth and I returned to Ithaca. A few days later, I came home from downtown to find Anne on the upstairs phone with

*Abbe Smith, "Where Angels Fear to Tread," forthcoming in *Law Stories*, edited by Gary Bellow and Martha Minnow (Ann Arbor: University of Michigan Press, 1995).

Abbe. She told me that Abbe had received a call from Roy Keefer, the D.A. for Adams County. He wanted us to come to Gettysburg, the county seat, next week to participate in a "discovery hearing," which he said was standard procedure.

Technically, the district attorney is a representative of "the people." She or he functions as an agent of the victim of a crime only if the victim's interests coincide with the primary interest of the district attorney's office: prosecution. Some prosecutors expend more effort than others safeguarding the concerns of victims, but that is due to personal convictions or awareness on their part, or the assertiveness of the victim and her family, or serendipity. The D.A.'s resources are dedicated toward the single goal of convicting criminals.

All of this became clear as Abbe explained what "discovery" was. A discovery hearing is a full exploration of the crime and the events surrounding it, in which both the district attorney and the attorney for the defense are allowed to cross-examine the witnesses so that they can decide how to proceed with the case. A hearing is not much different than a trial, according to Abbe, minus opening and closing arguments and a jury.

Roy Keefer clearly had no idea that Rebecca's sisters had been grappling since her death with how to tell their father that she and I had been lovers. They hadn't done it yet, and it was impossible for the hearing to take place before Leon Wight knew that his oldest daughter had been in a lesbian relationship. Mr. Wight would surely be at the hearing. He could not learn about our relationship for the first time in court.

I felt up against a wall. Boxed in and scared. Abbe, however, did not have my same sense of perpetual panic. She knew that court proceedings can be postponed. She said that she would do everything possible to make the Adams County judiciary see that this one needed to be.

Despite Abbe's assurances, I was shaken. I called Kevin Berrill from NGLTF and spoke to him directly for the first time that evening. The deep voice that consoled and advised me was to become, in the months ahead, a bedrock in my life. Kevin told me he shared Abbe's conviction that the inflexible system could be moved, that proceedings were routinely postponed. He also spoke with me about other cases of antigay violence, some of them murder. Without realizing it, Kevin was breaking the isolation I had experienced as a survivor. *This had happened to other people.* I was not utterly alone.

Abbe called back the next day and told us that she had talked to Roy Keefer and had gotten the discovery hearing postponed by one week. We still needed to go to Gettysburg on the sixteenth, however, because they had scheduled a lineup and a meeting of the prosecution team for that day. Evelyn and Judy, Rebecca's sisters, had one week to speak with their dad.

One afternoon during the intermediate days, I was alone in the house for the first time. My ever-present anxiety had subsided slightly. I was sitting in the living room when I heard clatter on the back porch. No one was expected. I jumped up with my heart pounding and moved carefully to where I could see onto the porch. It was two boys, maybe ten years old, who had decided to steal the five-cent returnable cans that had collected there. As I chased them, shouting, I knew my scolding was way out of proportion.

The evening before the lineup, Denny drove from Harrisburg to Ithaca to pick up Anne and me. The D.A.'s office was being very protective. I was wound up, thinking about seeing and pointing out Rebecca's killer, as the three of us sped down Route 81 in Denny's unmarked car.

We stayed at a motel in Gettysburg that night, right across from a Civil War battlefield. Denny was sensitive to how nervous I was, both about the ID and in general. He carefully acknowledged my fears and slept in the room next door to ours, just to be there. He told us to call him for anything. His concern was above and beyond having me feel safe enough to identify his perpetrator the next day; it seemed to be a part of Denny's nature. I also thought that after spending so much time with Anne and me and the rest of our family, he rather enjoyed our company.

We swam in the pool out in front of the motel, where Don Blevins' son was employed as a lifeguard. I was sure everyone in this small world knew who I was, and I felt very vulnerable. Abbe and Nancie met us later and also spent the night so they would be there for the early morning procedures. Abbe reassured me over and over that I would have no trouble identifying Carr. I had seen him, she told me. I had seen him, I told myself. But I was terrified that somehow I would make a mistake. Tomorrow's task seemed the most important on earth.

The next morning, the five of us met Don Blevins and Roy Keefer at the state police barracks. Roy Keefer was in his late thirties, with wavy auburn hair. He looked like he would rather have been wearing a sport shirt and slacks than the blue three-piece suit and tie he had on. He had glasses with dark plastic rims. When I talked with him I sensed that although we might not completely agree with each other's politics, he was not going to be homophobic.

Stephen Roy Carr's attorney was there also, just him alone with the seven people from "our team." The Adams County Public Defender's office was only staffed by a half-time position, and they had had to hire someone from the outside to take on Carr's defense. Michael George was in his early thirties, with short hair and a smooth handshake. He was slightly slick in a small-town way, and moderately pleasant when we exchanged hello's.

I knew Michael George was on Stephen Roy Carr's side; I knew he was going to try to defend Carr in whatever way he could. And he was going to do that because, in this country, people have the right to an attorney no matter how guilty they obviously are.

The "system" had been almost all-embracing of me thus

far. I had found compassion in the hospital staff at Hershey who had made me feel safe, had willingly contacted my chosen family, and let them, not just blood relatives, stay with me twenty-four hours a day. There was benevolence in Denny and Don, who had believed my story, who had worked eighteen-hour days to find the murderer. In Lew, who had trusted my intuition in making the composite. In the progressive community in Ithaca which had reached out to meet my needs, providing money and support. And in Abbe and Roy, who had postponed the hearing by another week so that Rebecca's sisters could come out on her behalf to their father.

It was only much later that I realized what an unusual experience I had had. It's not that my family and I didn't know that at any point the health care or criminal justice systems could have been extremely homophobic. We understood that homophobia is built into them. We were very aware of it, and we prepared for it constantly. Yet it didn't happen. If Rebecca and I had been a straight couple, all the things that had gone well would have been just normal. Gratitude for what others take for granted is a commentary on the oppressiveness of homophobia.

So I was not on the lookout for malevolence in Gettysburg. When we met, Stephen Roy Carr's lawyer said he was sorry about what had happened to me. Face to face, Michael George was never anything but polite. I forgot that to Mr. George, I was not a survivor of a violent crime; I was the opposition's prime witness.

We all went into the two-sided chamber where the lineup was to take place. The lighting was dim in our half, but a large window, which was in reality a one-way mirror, looked into a brightly lit box of a room on the other side. As in the hospital a month before when Denny had wanted me to identify Carr in the decade-old picture, a tape recorder was on and he formally noted the date, time, location, and people present. Abbe was at my elbow, Anne nearby. With Denny, Roy Keefer, and Michael George, we filled up the space. Five men filed into the other room and stood with their backs to the wall, their faces toward us. It was very quiet.

I noticed immediately that all five of the white men had dramatically different body types. One of them, the second from the left, was very gangly, his spindly legs so long that they seemed out of proportion, making his waist too high on his body. Even the next tallest of the other men was much shorter than he. Had height alone been the identifying characteristic, Stephen Roy Carr would still have stood out among the others.

I stared at the face atop that body to be sure it was one I recognized. Its lumps and hollows gave him a mongrel look, somewhere between Neanderthal and famine survivor. His forehead protruded over his eyes, which were small and deeply recessed. Most of the rest of his face was taken up by sunken checks and a narrow jawline. When I had seen him on the trail, his hair had been long and he had had a scraggly beard and mustache. He had been cleaned up in jail—Denny told us that his body and clothes had been filthy when they brought him into custody—and had been given a haircut and shave.

Looking at him produced instant revulsion in me. I barely needed the time they gave me, nor the instructions to have each person turn to profile position. I pointed him out immediately, and my words were noted in the record. I was relieved. Then Denny told me that they needed a vocal ID as well.

I had never even heard of a vocal ID. The five men were taken out of view, and they each in turn said the phrases, "Are you lost already?" and "See you later." This was a little more difficult, and I listened mostly to the tone of the men's voices. Who was trying to not sound like himself? Who sounded like he didn't want to speak at all?

When I picked out Stephen Roy Carr's voice correctly, Michael George said to Roy Keefer, "You've got a good witness."

"I don't have a good witness," Roy said. "I have a great witness."

Then it really was over. A weight and a tension left me. I did not want even the smallest part of the prosecution to go awry, and anxiety welled up in me each time I had to participate in it. But after all the worry, the ID had been easy. I had seen him and, as Lew Trowbridge had told me, people just don't look that much alike. Stephen Roy Carr, in particular, was strange-looking, even with a haircut and cleaned up.

Some part of me must have been terrified to actually see him again. However, I wasn't going to let anything get in the way of sending the man who had willfully killed my lover to prison. I was also surrounded by people I trusted, and Carr was on the other side of a one-way mirror, guarded by police officers with guns. I never had to interact with him, and that was the way I wanted it. Seeing him made Rebecca more dead. I felt a deep and profound disdain for him, a feeling so devoid of respect that it thinned to a sharp, hard point of contempt. The next time I would have to be in the same room with him would be in court.

The prosecution team drove over to the courthouse. We had to meet in the conference room because we couldn't fit in Roy's office. Anne, Abbe, Nancie, and myself, Roy Keefer, the Adam's County Victim's Representative, and four police officers all sat around a long conference table.

Besides Denny and Don, the other two officers were John Holtz, who was tall, rugged, and broad, and Matt O'Brien, smaller, thin, and wiry. The two investigators I hadn't met until then, though friendly, both struck me as hard. Compared with Denny and Don, these men seemed calloused, armored by their experience of a world filled with criminals.

After introductions, one of them got right to the point. Stephen Roy Carr had said he had seen us "eat each other out." The two tough officers shifted in their chairs and rubbed their faces. Then the one who hadn't spoken explained that they needed to know if we had. He was sorry to have to ask, but probing into that bit of my private life would confirm that Carr was at the scene; Stephen Roy Carr would have had to have watched us to know what we had done. It would totally discredit his story that he thought he was shooting at deer, or if he tried to go back to saying he wasn't there at all.

For me, compared to the traumatic invasions my life had suffered, this was hardly an intrusion.

"Yes," I said. "Rebecca was having oral sex with me just before the first shots. It wasn't both ways, though."

Their collective sigh of relief was audible, the unpleasant task done with. Having this fact out in the open locked down another piece of the prosecution.

The meeting lasted for a long while after that, mostly talking strategy. A lot of "debriefing" happened too, with the officers sharing information about the investigation with us. Abbe and Roy hypothesized about how Michael George was going to try to make the case a "gay issue," and how we weren't going to do that. This was murder, and Roy made it clear that that was how he was going to prosecute the case.

Roy told us that it was no different than if it had been he and his wife lying by that stream. The bullets Carr shot into our bodies were no less painful or deadly because we were two women. It is not an issue of sexuality or privacy, he insisted, but murder. Roy decided to charge Carr with both murder and attempted murder, and he chose to try it as a capital case—one in which the maximum potential sentence is death.

Though Roy Keefer was correct in his assessment that murder is murder, pain is pain, no matter who the victims, we all realized that this crime probably would not have been committed against a heterosexual couple. Had it been Roy and his wife making love on that green tent fly on that beautiful day, in all likelihood, no one would be dead.

ˌ FIVE ˌ

ccording to Truman Capote in *In Cold Blood*,[*] "sane" people murder for money or power or revenge. Insane people murder over some fantasied slight, in a moment of unreality, or because they are sociopaths, acting without regard for good or evil. Did Stephen Roy Carr fit into one of these two categories?

Carr had been convicted of numerous other crimes, but had never murdered anyone before. This time, he loaded a bullet into the action of his rifle, took aim at Rebecca and me, and pulled the trigger. As I started screaming, he lifted the bolt of the gun, pulled it back, put another bullet in the barrel, snapped the bolt closed, took aim, and fired. He did this six more times. Hours after the shooting, he told John Gulden that he had done a bad thing. Then he ran and hid because he did not want to get "put away for a long time." He cried when the police told him that they had found his belongings at the murder scene and that I had lived.

Stephen Roy Carr's actions were not those of a crazy person. He did not laugh uncontrollably or walk calmly away or claim that he heard the Devil talking in his ears. He knew that what he had done was wrong and that there were serious consequences to his actions. He fit legal and psychological definitions of sanity.

[*] Truman Capote, *In Cold Blood* (Random House, 1966).

His motive for murder was not money or revenge. Perhaps it was about jealousy or power. As low on the social ladder as Carr was—being a disconnected drifter, a social misfit with no community, no money, no home, with only a string of mistakes, misdeeds, and failures behind him—he may have believed that as a white, heterosexual man, he was higher up than a lesbian. He could not have articulated this analysis of the power structure of U.S. society, but it served as a backdrop for the twisted thinking that could find the murder of two lesbians a "reasonable" course of action.

Without doubt, Stephen Roy Carr was the product of our homophobic society. Most major cultural institutions in America—the family, organized religion, the law, psychology, mass media—make invisible or condemn homosexuality. Despite high divorce rates and mounting awareness about child abuse within the traditional heterosexual family, marriage and raising children are still held up as the greatest good. Gays and lesbians cannot legally marry; our relationships and families are routinely ignored.

The messages about homosexuality from most religious denominations are, at best, two-faced. In a recent Vatican statement, the Catholic Church denounced "violent malice in speech or in action" against gays, but then went on to blame such malice or antigay violence on the gay rights movement:

> When civil legislation is introduced to protect behavior to which no one has any conceivable right, neither the Church nor society at large should be surprised when other distorted notions and practices gain ground, and irrational and violent reactions increase.*

Statements like this condoning or sympathizing with violent hatred of lesbians and gays can be heard from the pulpits of

*Vatican Statement, "Congregation for the Doctrine of the Faith" (1986).

all but the most progressive groups of Christians, Jews, and Muslims. Homophobia disguised as "acceptance"—when the Conservative Jewish movement allowed lesbians and gays as members of congregations but forbade them from becoming rabbis, teachers or youth group leaders, for example—effectively adds to the contempt in which gay people are held.

The institutions of the American legal system reinforce the status of lesbians and gays as second-class citizens. Except in a handful of cities and fewer states, it is legal to discriminate on the basis of sexual orientation in employment and housing. Stores, hotels, and restaurants can legally refuse service to an openly gay person. Twenty-four states and the District of Columbia retain sodomy laws established several hundred years ago that the Supreme Court continues to uphold. The federal government has refused to pass basic civil rights legislation for gay and lesbian people. "Such governmental action (and inaction) clearly conveys the message that lesbians and gay men do not deserve full legal protection and justice. It also signals to perpetrators, criminal justice personnel, and the rest of society that antigay hate crimes will not be punished."*

While homosexuality was removed from the American Psychiatric Association's standard diagnostic manual in 1974, twenty years later, some mental health professionals and much of the public still thinks of homosexuality as a "disease" needing a "cure." In mainstream culture—television, movies and books—lesbians and gays are rarely depicted and even less frequently shown in a positive light. With few exceptions, gay male characters are the opposite of the hero: wimpy, sniveling, laughable, or evil. Lesbian characters are in sharp contrast to the ingenue: aggressive, man-hating, ugly, or evil. Even in cartoons, says media analyst Vito Russo, "...characters whose homosexuality is implied through their violation of gender roles long have been targeted for ridicule, contempt, and violence."** What is

*Berrill and Herek, p. 293.
**p. 92.

most common, however, is that the "heterosexual assumption" prevails, and homosexual characters in the media are simply invisible.

In almost all school districts, gay and lesbian teachers remain closeted for fear of being fired. Antigay jokes are acceptable in classrooms where Jews or women or African-Americans are no longer considered allowable targets. Books and discussions in health classes largely ignore bisexuality or homosexuality, and if the conservatives had their way, school districts that teach anything positive about a gay or lesbian lifestyle would lose their funding.

The norms and ethics of these all-pervasive institutions shape people's social and personal morals. When a city councilperson from Wilkes-Barre (a small city in Pennsylvania near the site of the shooting)—a sophisticated and educated man compared to Stephen Roy Carr—is quoted as saying that half of all gays should be shot and that AIDS is just what gay people deserve, and a Broward County (Florida) Circuit Judge jokingly asks the prosecuting attorney in a 1988 case involving the beating death of an Asian-American gay man, "That's a crime now, to beat up a homosexual?", is it any wonder perpetrators believe that lesbians and gay men are justifiable targets?[*]

>

On Thursday morning, June 23, the courthouse in Gettysburg was filled with many faces from my life. Kris, Karen, Nancie, Anne. Denny, Don, Matt O'Brien, John Holtz. Leon and Evelyn Wight. Abbe, sitting with me as always, at my left elbow. Reporters. And a lot of people I didn't know—the public. All of us were behind the sculpted wooden rail separating us from the legal players.

Stephen Roy Carr had been led in by two guards, in leg

[*]Berrill and Herek, p. 294.

irons and handcuffs. In front of the mahogany bar were the court reporter, the judge behind his elevated stand, Roy Keefer seated at one long wooden table, and Michael George and Carr, now unshackled, at the other. Abbe and I sat just behind Roy Keefer, close enough to see the stitching on the back seam of his grey suit. Uniformed bailiffs, standing at ease, were sprinkled liberally at all exits around the courtroom.

I hardly looked at Stephen Roy Carr. He sat resting his head in his right hand and stared at the table. He seemed blank to me. Vacant, stupid, unimpressive, ugly in blue prison garb which was too short for him at the arms and ankles.

Michael George stood and began. "Good afternoon, Your Honor. I'd like to enter my appearance on behalf of the Defendant Stephen Carr. We'll plead not guilty to all counts."

Roy stood too. There was some discussion about how the witnesses were to be sworn in. Then Judge Deardorff, an older white man in a black robe, announced, "I shall enter a plea of not guilty and we're ready to proceed."

I was to be called to the stand first. Roy was concerned about me and had said to Abbe, "Make sure she has her medicine." About two weeks before, I had had a long telephone conversation with my first woman lover who was now a naturopathic physician. I had told her how disconnected from the earth I felt. The next day, she Fed-Ex'ed a bottle of arsenicum extract, a homeopathic remedy for panic. Minutes after I dissolved two tablets under my tongue, I felt better. A day later, I was grounded, and I had been taking the remedy ever since. Roy didn't care what homeopathy was, he just wanted me to have anything I needed on the stand. I took some arsenicum in a glass of water with me when Roy called my name.

I was sworn in, and Roy asked me a few questions about where I currently lived, my study abroad last year, and then how Rebecca and I knew each other.

"About a year and a few months ago," I said, "Rebecca and

I became involved in a relationship that included a romantic component, a sexual component, and a friendship component. From last March until her death we were involved in that kind of intimate relationship, a lesbian relationship where we kept in touch throughout my journey to Israel and upon my return." Deliberate use of the word *lesbian*. We wanted to show that we weren't afraid of the issue.

"At some point, Claudia, did you and Rebecca make plans to come here to Adams County in the spring of this year?"

I replied that we had arranged to meet halfway between Ithaca and Blacksburg to go camping. Roy asked whether I had been camping before.

"Yes. Many, many times. By myself and with Rebecca."

I was conscious of the courtroom full of people, but at the same time, I was just answering questions that Roy and I both knew the answers to. I almost never took my eyes off of him. He led me through the story of May 12, up to the morning after seeing Carr. I described how Rebecca and I had spent that morning:

"...made hot water, ate breakfast, sat around, talked about the day, talked about things, just had a nice morning. It was a beautiful day, very warm."

"What did you decide to do at that point?" asked Roy.

"We looked at the map, and since we had—our original intention was to take a day hike—"

"What does that mean? What is a day hike?"

"That means you leave your tent set up at the campsite and you just take a small knapsack and maybe some food and go for a day hike and then come back and sleep at the same place," I explained. "But since there was another individual at the campsite, and we had really gone to have a little bit of a weekend together, it just seemed like, why not take everything, take a hike and see if there was a nicer campsite."

"The two of you wanted to be alone?" said Roy.

"Correct. In fact, the entire time I was at the campsite,

from the point when Rebecca came back to the point when we packed up, I thought nothing about whether there was another individual there. Assuming he was there to enjoy the campsite like I was, and I had no particular interest in meeting him and continued on with my life. So as we packed up the campsite, we both noticed that he was still there. When we left, I saw him sitting in the lean-to."

"How far away were you from this person?"

"Perhaps twenty or thirty feet, I'm not sure."

"You didn't measure it?" Roy quipped.

"Right."

He asked me to describe how Stephen Roy Carr had been sitting in the lean-to, and what he had looked like.

And he finally asked, "Did you see the person's face?"

"Yes."

"Did you see the person's face to a point where you would recognize that face if you saw it again?"

"Yes."

"Is the person you saw that day sitting in the lean-to present in the courtroom today?"

"Yes," I said.

"Could you point that person out, please?"

"Sitting with his attorney at the end of the table."

"The gentleman in the blue shirt?"

"Yes."

"Your Honor," Roy said, "I would ask that the record reflect that the witness has identified the Defendant in this case, Mr. Stephen Carr."

Judge Deardorff nodded. "Okay, so recorded."

Roy turned back to me. "Did you or Rebecca have any conversation with the Defendant as you walked past him at that point?"

"We said 'See you later.' Kind of a standard acknowledging of another human being present."

"Kind of like, 'Have a nice day'?"

"See ya, yeah," I said.

"Did you really expect to see him again?" Roy asked.

"Never."

Then I talked about the rest of the day—hiking, meeting Carr again on the trail, finding the beautiful campsite off the Rocky Knob Trail, making iced tea.

Roy asked me, "During all that time period, had you seen anyone else at all?"

"Absolutely nobody."

"Had you heard anyone else, any noises in the woods that would seem as if there were people around?"

"Nothing. I believed we were completely alone."

"What happened next, Claudia?"

"What happened was, when we were laying down—and as I said to you, we were involved in a relationship together, so we were affectionate together. There was talking. There was laughing. There was kissing. There was playfulness. There was making love. There was sexual activity, and it was very enjoyable. There was sun shining and the stream beside the campsite. It was as if any couple was enjoying an afternoon together by a stream."

"How long were you there at the stream before things began to happen differently?"

"I think I estimated that the first shot was fired about 5:30, so my guess is that it was forty-five minutes to an hour."

Roy then pulled a lot of details from me about the shooting. When I couldn't remember, I said that, although most things were very clear in my memory. We reached the point when I was deciding to leave the campsite, to leave Rebecca.

"It was obvious to you at that point that Rebecca was hurt a lot more than you were?"

"Yes."

"She was, in fact, dying?"

"Probably. I had thought I would die, and somewhere when I was holding that towel on my neck, I suddenly realized, I can live. You know, I am going to live, unless I got shot again, which of course, I was thinking that."

"You were still worried about that at that point?"

"At any second I was going to get shot at again," I said.

Roy questioned me for a few more minutes about getting out of the woods and getting help, and then gave the questioning over to Michael George.

"Miss Brenner, on how many occasions between the time of the incident and until today have you talked with the police?"

"Many."

"Can you tell me how many?"

"Not exactly."

"More than ten?"

"Probably, yes."

"More than twenty?"

"Probably."

"Each time you spoke with them, did you give them a statement of what you could remember?"

"I always told them whatever I could. First to help them catch the guy who shot us, and then whatever help they wanted to work on the case. Yes."

He asked me whether I had seen pictures of Carr before the visual ID last week. I acknowledged that I had seen his picture in the newspaper. It was nearly impossible not to, as the arrest was on the front page in my hometown and a lot of other places, too.

Then he suddenly asked, "Did you at any time indicate to the police that there may be somebody else threatening your life or threatening your friend's life?"

"Never."

"Had either of you been married?"

"No."

I didn't think about the *why* of his line of questioning while I was on the stand. I just answered honestly. Roy and Abbe had told me to expect questions that seemed unrelated to the case.

He asked how often I had spoken with Roy and what role Abbe had been playing in the case. Then he began lining up for his approach.

"The morning of May 13, you say that you got up at sunrise, approximately, and you were the first one out of the tent?"

"Correct. I just went outside to go to the bathroom and went right back inside of the tent."

"And you had no clothing on, correct?"

"Correct."

"Did you go toward the lean-to area?"

"No."

"You went away from there?"

"I went a little bit away to go to the bathroom. I didn't go to the outhouse." I explained the layout of the campsite.

Michael George continued. "At some point, Rebecca got out of the tent?"

"Correct."

"Until that occasion when she got out of the tent to go to the bathroom, had either of you left the tent again?"

"She might have gone out of the tent and just gone to the bathroom close by the tent, like I did, once. I am not really certain. But she saw nobody."

"Inside the tent I assume that you and your friend were being intimate again?"

"Inside the tent, prior to Rebecca going to the outhouse, we didn't see anyone and we were being intimate."

Roy and Abbe and I had gone over ways to reduce the heat of inflammatory statements, like reiterating our points and answering his provocative questions as an afterthought.

"Kissing, rolling over with each other, making love?"

"The things that people who are in love do with each other." Nothing to take apart. Not a sordid confession.

"At some point, then, Rebecca got up and left the tent to go outside?"

"Right."

"At this point, Rebecca, again, didn't have any clothing on?"

"Correct. We completely believed we were alone until the point when Rebecca came upon your Defendant."

"When she went up to the outhouse, how long was she up there?"

"Four or five minutes maybe."

"Were you inside or outside the tent?"

"I think I had started to boil water on the stove outside the tent."

"Again, you were naked?"

"Right."

"Did you watch Rebecca as she went up to the outhouse?"

"I saw her leave, and then I started boiling water to make coffee and that was the last I thought about it. I was just sitting by the campsite."

"On any occasion did you see her speaking with anyone?"

"No. I only know she spoke with him because she came back and told me."

"When she came back, she didn't have any clothing on?"

"Correct, but then she put on clothing immediately and so did I."

"Your Honor," Michael George protested, "I am going to ask you to instruct the witness to please answer my questions. I think she intends to keep going through the narratives."

Roy interrupted, "Your Honor, she did answer the question."

Judge Deardorff agreed. "I feel she answered the question that was asked."

For the third time Michael George asked, as if running through a tricky step in a logic proof, "When she came back from going to the outhouse, she did not have any clothing on, correct?"

"Correct." Then being completely accurate, I said, "Sneakers."

"So, to the best of your knowledge, while she was speaking to this person, she was completely naked?"

"Correct."

"After she came back from the outhouse, is it true that you two began fondling each other again?"

Fondling? "I believe that at some point during the rest of the morning, which was about two hours long, there were times when we embraced and kissed, as people who love each other do. I don't recall if it was immediately upon her return. What I recall was that immediately upon her return she said, 'We're not alone, let's put on some clothes.' And I said, 'Yes,' and I put on some clothes, she put on some clothes, and we proceeded with breakfast."

"What clothes did you put on?"

"I put on shorts and a T-shirt, and she put on jeans and a T-shirt."

"After she had informed you that there was somebody else present, you still went on, as you would say, caring for each other, fondling each other, kissing each other?"

"I would say we had breakfast and we were in the area of the campsite for another several hours and proceeded with our lives. Which sometimes included embracing and kissing, which didn't mean we were laying outside of the tent together."

Michael George seized on the words. "Kissing, embracing. Were you feeling each other?"

"Excuse me?"

Had I thought to look out into the court beyond Michael George's impassive face, I would have seen Abbe scribbling furiously on the yellow legal pad in front of her. Torn pages were folded and handed to Roy in silence.

Michael George repeated, "Were you feeling each other?"

"Feeling?"

"With hands, yes."

"Not to any great extent at that point."

"Were you aware that my client was in the area at this point?"

"I believed him to be minding his own business in his lean-to. A good distance away."

"Could you or could you not see him?"

"I could not see him."

"You left some two hours later, is that correct?"

"Several hours, yes."

"You passed which way, in front of the lean-to, or you left away from the lean-to?"

"You have to pass right by it. You walk up the trail and it's to your left."

Then Michael George went into his final descent. "At some point, did either you or your friend lift your shirt and sort of show?"

"No."

"No?"

(I later learned that Abbe's note at this point read: "Roy, don't you think this is getting out of hand?")

"No, absolutely not," I replied.

"Did either of you make any other comments to my client outside of what you've testified to?"

"No."

"Were you walking hand in hand?"

"Not at that point."

"Were you walking hand in hand at any point near the lean-to?"

"No."

"At all times during that two-hour period before you left the initial camp, were you and Rebecca in constant sight of each other?"

"Yes."

"She never left again to go to the bathroom?"

"I don't believe so."

"You're saying yes, or you're saying no, that didn't happen, or no, you don't know whether or not that happened?"

"At some point we washed the dishes down at the stream. I think we both went down there together. We packed up the tent. I think I walked off into the brush again to urinate at one point where she may not have been directly in my sight, but she didn't have any other contact with any other people."

"To the best of your knowledge?"

"To the best of my knowledge," I granted, "which was within fifteen or sixteen feet away."

"At any time after you put your clothing on until you left, did you undress in any way?"

"I don't think so. At one point when I was laying down, I might have let my stomach get in the sun's rays, but I didn't take my shirt off."

Then Michael George asked a few questions about seeing Carr at the intersection of the trail, before he got to the site of the shooting itself.

"When you got to your second campsite, was it at that point that you undressed again?"

"We had something to eat. We sat by the campfire. We talked. We made iced tea. We drank cold water."

"Would you please answer my question. Did you or did you not undress?"

I said that my shorts and only Rebecca's sneakers were off.

"What, actually, were you doing?" Michael George asked.

I had been waiting for this. "As I described to Mr. Keefer, we were engaged in making love. There was some oral sex involved. There was kissing. There was rolling around playfully and there was affection."

"Would you define oral sex for me?" Michael George asked.

That, I was not prepared for. Even so, I looked directly at him and said, "Oral sex is when one person has their mouth on someone else's genitals."

More questions about where and when and if we had "fondled" each other, by the stream, at the other campsite.

"At any point during that afternoon, to your knowledge, did either you or Rebecca put on a show for my client?"

"No." Definite.

"At any time during that day, did you, or to the best of your knowledge, Rebecca, intentionally tease my client?"

"No." Firm.

"At any point during that entire day, did either you, or to the best of your knowledge, Rebecca, purposely reveal any parts of your body to my client?"

"No." Adamant.

"Prior to the incident, had either of you had, for lack of a better term, a falling out with a female lover of any sort?"

"No."

"At any point did you tell the police there may be somebody who had threatened to kill you before?"

"Never."

"Were you scared of anybody because—"

"Never. Never scared of anyone trying to hurt me."

"Because of a broken romance of any sort?"

"Never scared of anyone trying to hurt me, ever."

"How about, to the best of your knowledge, was Rebecca?"

"Never scared of anyone trying to hurt her."

"Of course that applies to both male and female?"

"Correct. Never frightened of anyone trying to hurt us."

"To your knowledge, were the police interested in any other relationship that you may or may not have had?"

I was ready to answer, although I wasn't sure exactly what the question was, but Roy jumped in. "Objection, Your Honor. It calls for conclusions on the part of the witness. It's beyond the scope of direct examination. If he wants to ask those questions of the police, that's fine. To ask the witness what she thought the police thought is ridiculous."

Michael George said, "I'll withdraw the question. Did the police ever question you about any prior relationships?"

"They only were questioning me to solve the crime."

"Does that mean yes or no?"

"No."

He was finally done.

Roy came back and clarified a few points about the lineup and vocal IDs, which Michael George had briefly mentioned. Then he asked, "Claudia, when those shots were fired, and you knew you were shot, and you knew Rebecca was shot, was there any thought of anyone else in your mind who could possibly want to do that to you, other than the Defendant?"

"Absolutely not."

Michael George challenged me about that when he got to recross-examine me, and I repeated that I knew that it was Carr who had shot us because I had seen him with a gun and he was the only person who might have known where we were. That questioning lasted only a few minutes, and then the defense was finished with me, and so was Roy, and the judge excused me from the stand.

I sat back down, slightly dazed, next to Abbe. I had forgotten to expect such sleazy tactics and was too startled by Michael George's relentless quest for the sordid to be outraged yet. I just sat quietly and watched as Roy called Don Blevins to the stand.

Don told about looking for and finding Rebecca's body six weeks before. After that, Rebecca's father went up. Evelyn and Judy had told him and their stepmother about Rebecca being a lesbian, and the full story of the shooting, the previous week.

He seemed to be handling the information. To my relief, his anger was directed at Stephen Roy Carr and not at me.

"Mr. Wight," Roy said, "I realize this may be difficult for you. I am going to show you a photograph that's been marked as Commonwealth's exhibit number one, and ask you to take a look at the person depicted in that photograph and identify for the court, please, if you know, who that person is?"

Leon Wight looked at the photograph held out by Roy Keefer and said, "That is my dead daughter, Rebecca."

Michael George did not cross-examine Leon Wight. There was no way for him to distort the identification of a father's daughter shot dead in the woods.

Don, who was to return to the stand several more times during the hearing, was recalled. Roy used his testimony to note for the court what the autopsy report on Rebecca said. Don read aloud: "...wounds...chest and abdomen...demise...homicide."

After some legal wrangling with Michael George over the use of the coroner's report rather than his appearance in court, Roy called the Guldens' teenage son to the stand. The boy seemed less than happy about being there.

"State your name for the record, please."

"John Wayne Gulden."

"How old are you, Mr. Gulden?"

"Seventeen."

"Mr. Gulden, are you familiar with the Defendant in this case, Mr. Stephen Carr?"

"Yeah."

"How long have you known Mr. Carr?"

"Most of my life."

"Is he a friend of the family?"

"Yeah."

"Has Mr. Carr been a visitor in your home on occasions prior to this incident taking place?"

"Yeah."

"Specifically, Mr. Gulden, did you have an opportunity to speak with the Defendant, Stephen Carr, on the morning of Saturday, May 14, 1988?"

"Yeah."

"Where did that conversation take place?"

"In my kitchen."

"Of your home?"

"Yeah."

"So Mr. Carr was apparently visiting at that time?"

"Yeah."

"Do you recall, had he been there the day before on the thirteenth?"

"No."

"You don't recall or he had not been?"

"He had not been."

"The conversation with Mr. Carr—what did he say to you, please?"

"All I can remember is I just woke up, and he said, 'I did something wrong,' and I was gone."

"He said what?" asked Roy.

"'I did something wrong.' That's all I can remember." Then the teenager repeated that he had left the house.

A brief cross-examination by Michael George followed, and John Wayne Gulden was excused from the stand.

Roy questioned John Wayne's mother, Alice Gulden, about the shell casings the police obtained from her backyard. He recalled Don Blevins for a third time, to have him recount the search for evidence in the woods around the Appalachian Trail. Then John Holtz was sworn in.

"How long have you been a Pennsylvania state police officer, Trooper Holtz?" Roy asked.

"This fall I'll start my twenty-first year."

Jack Holtz's grey hair and height made him look dignified. The trooper told the court how he and Corporal O'Brien had, after Stephen Roy Carr's arrest, informed him of his rights, and that Carr had signed a waiver to defer them. They had made sure Carr could read what he was signing, and that he was not on drugs or drunk at the time. Then Trooper Holtz recounted how his questioning had evolved from asking about Stephen Roy Carr's life since he had left Florida, to his confession of pulling the trigger, to his taking the police to retrieve the gun.

Roy proceeded. "Did Mr. Carr make a statement during the time of transportation?"

"He did," confirmed Holtz.

"What was that statement, please?"

"Mr. Carr was asked if he really saw the girls kissing. Carr said the girls were lesbians. Carr said after he set up his camp at the creek, he saw the girls. They were engaged in a lesbian act. Carr said, and I quote, 'They were eating each other out.'"

"Did he mention," asked Roy, "anything about deer during that statement?"

"No, sir," said Holtz.

On cross-examination, Michael George queried Holtz about the officers' interrogation of Carr: whether they had taken notes (they hadn't, Holtz explained, since it wasn't customary); whether Carr had asked at any time for an attorney (he hadn't); and whether Trooper Holtz had ever gone to seminars or trainings on proper interrogation techniques (he had, in fact, taught some).

George repeatedly brought up Carr's statement that he had seen "the girls" kissing, trying to make the time reference appear ambiguous. Couldn't Carr have meant the morning of the thirteenth instead of the evening? The questioning went around in circles, with Trooper Holtz stating that Carr clearly meant the evening, just before the shooting happened, and Michael George insisting he could have meant the morning.

On his opportunity to redirect, Roy asked a few more questions of John Holtz.

"Trooper Holtz, when the Defendant asked you for cigarettes, did he get some?"

"Yes. In fact, every time he asked, he was given a cigarette."

"How about when he asked for water. Did he get some of that?"

"Yes, and also when he asked for something to eat."

"Just one further question. In the seminars that you have been involved in, which Attorney George brought up, did you learn about what Miranda warnings are?"

"Yes."

"Did you learn when someone asks for an attorney, you stop questioning?"

"Immediately."

"Did that ever happen during the course of questioning Stephen Carr?"

"Not when myself or Corporal O'Brien were talking to him, no."

"Would you remember if it had, Trooper?"

"Yes. Because that would have been the last line in my report."

Don Blevins was recalled a final time to discuss investigating the scene of the crime itself. He detailed how detectives under his supervision had strung a string in a continuous line from the area where the shots had originated, through graze marks on the laurel saplings, to the place, eighty-two feet away, where Rebecca and I had lain.

"Would it be fair to say that the entire area," asked Roy, meaning the line of fire, "is no more than two feet off the ground?"

"If you were to fire higher than two feet," said Don, "you would probably hit thicket. Two feet would be the maximum."

"Trooper Blevins, do you know of any two-feet-tall deer?"

"None that I'm aware of."

The Commonwealth had no further questions or witnesses. Stephen Roy Carr was not called to the stand. While in the courtroom, he never once said a word.

Before leaving Gettysburg the next morning, Kris, Karen, and I—Anne had left the day before, immediately after the hearing—bought the local papers and the *Philadelphia Inquirer* and read the articles about the hearing over breakfast. The articles were factual, with headlines that read: "Commonwealth Seeks Death Penalty for Carr" and "A Time of Terror When Gunshots Rang Out, Hiker Testifies."

We all felt that the hearing had gone well. Michael George didn't have an argument to stand on, and his two possible lines of defense contradicted each other: Stephen Roy Carr really hadn't meant to be shooting at Rebecca and me at all because he thought that we were a deer, and Stephen Roy Carr had been provoked to shoot us because of our lesbianism. The judge seemed at least neutral if not sympathetic. I had held up well on the stand, and the police were great, too.

For me, the hearing also made Rebecca more dead. With every event that happened—the media coverage, the line-up, the hearing, meeting Mr. Wight for the first time—she kept getting more and more and more dead. I was constantly stumbling over tenses. Every verb in every sentence, and even every thought, had to be changed. *Rebecca lives...lived there, we see ...saw each other often, we are...were lovers.* It was painful and awkward.

We drove back to Ithaca, digesting the court proceedings during the ride. Although Karen needed to return to Virginia soon to work on her dissertation, she was coming to Ithaca for a while longer, to spend time with me.

I remember that Kris pulled up to her house on Corn Street and got out to drop a few things off while Karen and I waited in the car. She stooped to pick up the folded newspaper on her porch, looked at the front page, gasped, and immediately returned to the car.

In bold, banner, one-inch type, the *Ithaca Journal* had headlined the story about the hearing, "WOMEN TEASED ME, MOUNTAIN MAN TESTIFIES." The Associated Press article under it used the words *sex, sex acts, lesbian* and *taunted* repeatedly. It referred to me as Rebecca's "Ithaca lover."

The sensationalism was bad enough. Besides that, it was flatly wrong. He hadn't testified. We hadn't teased him. And the press never refers to a partner in a heterosexual couple as a *lover*—it's always *companion* or *wife* or possibly, *boyfriend.* Unless it is the *National Enquirer* "reporting" on an affair, the sexuality in a straight relationship is a nonissue. But here our sexuality was in the lead paragraph, splashed all over my home town in a lurid headline.

One of us pulled out a five dollar bill, and Karen ran to the convenience store a half block away to buy all their papers. Kris and I raged in the car while we waited for her, but realized even as she turned the corner out of sight that her errand was futile. We could never buy all the papers in town, collect the ones delivered to people's homes, find those already bought from stands in the three hours since its release at noon that day.

When Karen returned with a stack of twenty or thirty papers, we threw the offending copies in the backseat and drove over to Wood Street. The household already knew by the time we arrived and they were furious. We felt betrayed. After everything we'd been through, did we also have to fight the local paper? People were calling the house, outraged. The photo editor at the *Ithaca Journal*, a friend, had phoned, saying that she had tried to get the headline changed before the paper went to press. She was sorry. Wood Street had been fuming since noon, and everyone was ready to stage an immediate protest at the *Journal*'s offices that afternoon.

I was scared. I didn't know what the effect of a protest would be on the case, and I was willing to forgo expressing my rage for a better chance at a Guilty outcome. I put in a call to Abbe, from whom we had parted just a few hours earlier.

Her advice was that everyone else should go full steam ahead, but that I should not be a visible part of any demonstrations, so as not to give the defense anything to use against me. Not radicalness, not political gain, not seeking attention or publicity. She was as indignant as the rest of us, but encouraged me to do my organizing behind the scenes. I thanked her and reported back what she had said.

Debating in the kitchen of Wood Street, we decided that the strength of a large, carefully orchestrated protest on Monday would outweigh the power of immediate rage. No matter how tempting instantaneous gratification seemed, we could use the weekend well to organize our supporters. Anne, Kris, Karen, and Gina began making phone calls and brainstorming ideas for street demonstrations.

My fury, however, was not going to smolder unabated for three days. I gathered two friends, one of whom was, calculatedly, a straight woman with a "good" job, your "average" taxpayer, well thought of in the community. When we strode in the front doors of the *Journal* building, a path opened up for us. Everyone there knew my face. We were directed upstairs to the city editor's desk.

The three of us made a classic scene. Our rhetoric was barbed, our fingers pointed. The editor eventually called in her supervisor, who eventually called the publisher.

The *Journal*'s top administrator was an African-American middle-aged woman, and I told her I couldn't believe that she would be so careless with a story about someone from another oppressed group. She and the two editors were all apologies and politic, committing to "do right by me" in the future, but skirting around actually promising to retract the headline. After a final gratifying harangue, I and my two backers turned and stormed back out the same path. The employees all stayed out of our way, staring at us.

Meanwhile, and throughout the weekend at the Wood and Corn Street houses, the phone receivers never rested in their cradles for more than a few moments. We called every dyke and dyke-friendly person in town that we knew, and asked them to talk to the people they knew. We had all been Ithaca residents for a long time, between ten and twenty years, and the gay community there was fairly large for a small town.

Over the weekend we used all the other networks we could think of to alert people to the action planned for Monday at three o'clock. Gina called her entire rugby team. I called people I used to work with at Family and Children's Service, the county Probation Department, and the Family Court. Satya was attending the Alternative Community High School, so we had connections there to staff, students, and their families. She also called friends from her after-school job as a manager at the Ithaca Ben and Jerry's store.

There were, too, all of those casual relationships that one acquires from living in the same place for a long time, relationships that one hardly thinks of in most situations. Not the people you invite to have dinner at your house, or come to a solstice celebration, but the people who make up your community: massage therapists, people seen at feminist events, acquaintances met in cafés and at the bank. We also contacted progressive organizations such as New Jewish Agenda, Ithaca Rape Crisis, the Moosewood restaurant collective, the two alternative weekly papers, and the *Cornell Daily Sun*.

The Sunday before the protest was my thirty-second birthday. Birthdays bring with them permission to be exactly how one wants. I didn't want a birthday. Rebecca was dead. I careened down from outrage to deep depression. I lay on the couch all day. The only gift I wanted was to see Anne's mime partner's two-year-old daughter, whose innocence I hoped would diminish my inner desolation. Barbara brought her over, but even her tiny smile couldn't penetrate my emptiness.

⸙

The shooting had been front-page news in Ithaca since it happened, and people talked about it all the time. Not just lesbians, everybody. Donations to the Claudia Brenner Fund at Family and Children's Service and support for my family relieved some of the feelings of helplessness, but none of the rage. By Monday, June 27, the community had been waiting five and one-half weeks to take on an embodiment of injustice.

At 2:45 P.M., the street in front of the small brick building that housed the *Journal* was crowded with men and women. Following Abbe's advice, I stayed home, with Anne keeping me company. She was grateful for an excuse to rest.

Some of the protesters were holding signs that read, "We don't want the National Enquirer for our news. We want RESPONSIBLE JOURNALISM." Some were talking to the people next to them. Some were reading the paste-up boards showing the less biased coverage in Gettysburg, Philadelphia, and the Central Pennsylvania Valley. All were sweating while they waited; it was the beginning of a hot summer.

The protesters were instructed by police not to block the street, so the crowd was organized into two long lines of marchers on the sidewalk, connected by U-turns on each end. As they paced in opposite directions, people on the inside of the sidewalk brushed shoulders with those near the road. The elongated oval stretched for half a block in each direction on State Street.

People had been asked to bring their copy of the June 24 issue of the *Ithaca Journal*, and Gina had brought scores of extras, too, for those who had not gotten them on Friday, or people who had not been contacted about the demonstration but happened by and joined in. She stood outside the lines of marchers, handing out copies to those who needed them.

Gina was pregnant and nauseous. She had decided back in college to have a baby by the time she was twenty-seven, and when the midnight news of the shooting had reached Wood Street a month and a half ago, her intended sperm donor had already bought a plane ticket to come up from New Orleans. It had seemed almost absurd at that moment to pursue anything not directly related to the crisis, but when some of the initial panic had subsided, she had decided with Anne and me to just "go for it." So using a borrowed apartment in Hershey (and a not very scientific procedure involving a tampon applicator), Gina conceived with the first insemination on the Wednesday after the shooting. Outside the *Journal* that day, she felt none of the excitement of pregnancy, just hot and angry and ready to vomit.

As protesters neared the window of the newspaper's offices, they held up their copies of the paper, pressing the words "WOMEN TEASED ME" against the glass, and chanting, "Shame, shame, shame."

A petition was circulated:

> We protest the *Ithaca Journal*'s account of the hearing at which Stephen Roy Carr was ordered to stand trial for murder and assault. The headline on the June 24 lead story was inaccurate and misleading, presenting the questioning of a defense attorney as if it were sworn testimony. The article distorted the facts of the hearing which were accurately reported in other newspapers. The Ithaca Journal sensationalized the proceedings and blamed the victims of a heinous crime. As members of the Ithaca community, we express our outrage. We demand a correction of the inaccuracies and an editorial apology for the distortions.

After twenty minutes of walking and chanting, Karen,

Satya, and Gina positioned themselves around the ring of people at various points. They held open large, plastic garbage bags. As demonstrators passed by, they tore up the pages in their hands and stuffed the shreds to the bottom of the tall green sacks, reciting more refrains of condemnation.

On Tuesday, the petition was delivered to the newspaper with over two hundred signatures, three bags full of crumpled newsprint were dropped off at the recycling center, and the *Journal* itself covered the protest on the front page, with photos.

Although the *Journal* never did retract the headline, they honored their promise to report the case respectfully. Rebecca and I were *companions* in all future articles. There were no more misleading headlines. Over the next few weeks, the editorial page ran dozens of letters protesting the "Mountain Man" headline and the blame the victim mentality it encouraged. The paper also published several gay-positive features not long after the uproar. As the only non-university daily paper in a small town, the *Journal* had a virtual monopoly and was not going to lose enough readership over this explosion to shut them down. But they paid attention. The Ithaca gay, lesbian and bisexual community—and its allies—were strong, and were not going to allow one of its own to be exploited.

' SIX '

The depression which began on my birthday persisted. I was finally coming down from the thousand-hour adrenaline surge that had gotten me out of the woods and through the hospital, the police investigation, and the initial court appearances. My therapist had explained that a human's capacity for acute crisis was finite. Mine would begin to abate in six to eight weeks, she assured me. I believed her.

After the *Ithaca Journal* fiasco, the crisis did begin to recede slightly. I transitioned from acute crisis to protracted recovery. My feelings roiled as I simultaneously grieved Rebecca's death and coped with the trauma of the shooting. Now, however, there were brief glimpses of relief in between. I had some familiarity with Elizabeth Kubler Ross' stages of death and dying, and could occasionally categorize thoughts into one stage or another. But mostly that summer the feelings remained raw with little of the intellectual buffer provided by theories. Late every Friday afternoon brought pain, like a sore torn open repeatedly and never allowed to heal. I charted our footsteps on the map. I recounted the journey. No Friday at 6:00 P.M. passed without my noticing the time of Rebecca's death.

I knew I was in mourning, though I had never mourned before. Many months passed before I began to acknowledge the pain connected to my own near-death. Until then, the miracle of my survival was irrelevant. Losing Rebecca was not mitigated by any miracles. The chasm between near-death and death is infinitely wide.

My healing from the trauma came in stages. At the time, the strongest paradigm of recovery I had was from co-counseling. Re-evaluation Counseling (another name for co-counseling) is a method of peer counseling that teaches that hurts, small or as large as this one, are stored in our minds and bodies until they are released. When people cry, yell, or shake, they "discharge" that pain, allowing them to think clearly about their situation, solve their problems, and get on with their lives. The philosophy of RC is that humans know what they need to do to heal themselves, and with the help of good attention and safety from another person, everyone can do that healing. I had been part of the RC community for ten years, and Anne and Gina and many of my friends practiced co-counseling as well. Everyone encouraged me to have faith that I knew what I needed. The moments of relief I had from suffering helped me believe that we were moving in the right direction.

I tried to let every moment be guided by intuition. When my inside voices said, *Talk to someone*, I talked. When they said, *Cry*, I cried. I read books about death and dying that drew me to them. Where I went and who I saw was determined by my instinct and my emotions. I did whatever felt right.

Years later, when I read Judith Herman's *Trauma and Recovery*, I was able to look back to that time and understand some of what I was doing. Intuitively, I was trying to accomplish the tasks of recovery: to feel safe, to remember and mourn, to make some sense of the shooting, to fit it into my view of myself and the world, and to restore social connection.

Establishing safety was an arduous process. Even though my friends were exhausted and dealing with their own secondary trauma, as well as trying to maintain scraps of their regular lives, I got round-the-clock care from them. If I had had to bear my wounds in silence, as children in cases of abuse do, for example, the terror gripping my spirit might never have lifted.

The shooting was not a hushed-up topic in our house. No one pretended I would forget if we didn't talk about it. No one believed talking about it would make it hurt more. Sentences did not drop off uncomfortably: "That was before...." It didn't seem unusual that later we began to mark events by the date: "Your sister's son was born just after you got shot, Claudia."

The professionals I dealt with helped make me feel safer, too. Both Dr. Noori, the psychiatrist at Hershey, and my therapist in Ithaca reassured me that what I was feeling was normal, that it even had a name. Jumpy, irritable, scared, and distrustful were all expected states of Post-Traumatic Stress Disorder. Dr. Noori had also calmed my early fear that it was impossible to heal after suffering a trauma so severe, promising that my doubt itself was a good sign. Questioning my condition meant that I was not in denial about it. My therapist agreed with Dr. Noori that the turbulent feelings meant I was not defending against the trauma by staying in denial. I was accepting the real emotions that came with such a severe violation: pain, terror, depression, hyper-awareness, rage. I was already doing the work to heal.

The "work" meant constant talking. It began in the hospital and lasted for a long time. I needed to return to the moments of the shooting again and again in order to pay attention to every detail. I started telling the story of the shooting as soon as I could speak coherently. I didn't wait until I felt completely safe. Months, even years, after I had recounted the story innumerable times, I still had flashes of terror.

At the beginning, I was going to professional therapy twice a week, co-counseling daily with Jill, and occasionally with other people as well. Jill and I would sit in one or the other of our homes and chip at the images in my head—how he carried the gun, how the blood looked on the tarp, what it was like leaving Rebecca—and the sounds, the loudness of the bullets, our screams.

Even if I hadn't wanted and needed to talk all the time, I couldn't have helped it. It seemed as if everyone who ever knew me checked in during those months. I was appreciative of all the phone calls, but often overwhelmed. The attention both gave something to me and took something away. Every time someone made the shooting real for themselves by talking to me, I had to expend energy toward their understanding, to reassure *them* that I would be okay.

People were often clumsy around Rebecca's death and the shooting. Some said nothing at all, perhaps thinking that anything they said would be inadequate to how I must be feeling. Some said, "I couldn't have done it if it was me," which made me feel alienated—I wasn't Superwoman—and I felt forced to assure them that they, too, could have survived under the circumstances. Or they said, "This must be hard for you to talk about," which meant, "This is hard for me to talk about."

Mostly it didn't really matter what people said to me. Nothing made it better. Rebecca was still dead, and she kept on being dead, day after day. For a long time my first thought every morning was, *Rebecca's dead.* Standing in the supermarket line buying milk and laundry detergent, I would think about how nothing about Rebecca could ever change again. In the movies, death can be romantic. In real life, it is dull and choking, boring and empty in its repetition.

Only time and counseling lessened the pain, but genuine support that asked nothing from me helped me to bear it. I appreciated, "I'm so sorry," "It's so terrible," or being allowed to talk about whatever aspect of the shooting was currently "up," rather than filling the listener in. It felt good also when people honestly offered their assistance: "I can help you with this. Would you like me to?"

Because of the extraordinary dedication of my friends and
the generosity of the larger community, I was not expected to
deal with very much outside of personal healing. I did have to
confer about the case, and no week went by without conversations with Abbe, Roy, and Denny. The other two concerns were
moving and money. I was without income, supported by donations to the Claudia Brenner Fund at Family and Children's Service. But I had follow-up doctor's and dentist's visits to pay for,
Abbe's fees, bills from both hospitals. It was a lot of money, tens
of thousands of dollars.

If I had had to pay for all those bills from the donations alone,
the financial stress would have been greater. Fortunately the Pennsylvania Crime Victim's Compensation Fund allots up to thirty-
five thousand dollars to pay for medical, legal, and work loss
expenses for victims of violent crimes. I began organizing letters, bills, credit card slips, and cancelled checks for submission.
The money, however, was literally going to take years to come
through the bureaucracy. I negotiated an interim arrangement with
Hershey Medical Center for minimal bill payment to keep their
automatic collection unit at bay.

Then there was moving. Anne, Satya, and I were moving
from Wood Street to the house in Freeville where Gina lived,
about twelve miles outside of Ithaca. Anne and Gina had been
planning this for a while. Satya was going to be a senior in high
school in the fall and had gotten her driver's license. With Satya
more independent, moving to the country became practical.

I was moving with them. I wanted to be safe, and safe meant
Anne. If Anne had moved to the moon, I would have gone with
her. It was good timing. I was filled with compulsive energy
that could be well-channeled into the mundane and endless tasks
of packing and moving. Anne and Satya had lived at that house
in town for almost ten years, and the daughter had picked up
the mother's habit of never throwing anything away. We spent
July and August clearing out the basement, attic, shed, and clos-

ets, cleaning, and carting endless truckloads of stuff: to the dump, the Salvation Army, friends, and packed-up boxes to Freeville.

The big, yellow 1910 farmhouse had poor insulation, plaster that threatened to come down while you were sitting under it, and projects everywhere. But under the neglect, there was a solid frame with several beautiful windows, doors with hardwood frames and stained-glass borders, and lovely wainscotting. It was sited with views of the sunrise and sunset. Right before I had gone on the camping trip with Rebecca, I had begun to build a new set of stairs and a back porch. We were one board short of finishing the very bottom tread when I left. I intended to buy the last 2x6 when I came back from backpacking. The gaping hole that remained for weeks before we fixed it was yet another strange reminder of loss.

Abbe Smith and Roy Keefer were dancing through whatever legal moves were necessary. Michael George had shown his hand at the discovery hearing, and Abbe and Roy wanted to cut off the "homophobia panic defense" possibility for the trial. They eventually decided to file a motion that would prevent the defense from introducing evidence of my relationship with Rebecca. If successful, this would stop Michael George from arguing that Stephen Roy Carr's actions were the result of provocation.

As a former defense lawyer, Abbe had mixed feelings about her role reversal in aggressively working against a defendant. As a feminist and lawyer for me as the victim, she realized that there was no justification for using provocation as a defense.

Roy incorporated Abbe's research into his arguments at a hearing in September. The brief established that distaste for someone's "choice of lover" or "lawful sexual conduct" was not serious grounds for provocation.

➤

The more I told the story of the shooting, the less power it had over me, and the more my sense of safety grew. I told it and cried about it so many times that it eventually began to heal into a memory. As a memory, it could be integrated into my regular world. I began to make sense of the shooting as part of my life, my "self-story." Integration did not mean that I was in less pain, but I did feel less split off from myself. The shooting was not compartmentalized in my thoughts, isolated from the rest of my life. It was becoming a memory that was interwoven with everything else in my world, and that world was being transformed into a place where it was not inconceivable that I could be shot.

I grew up believing that I was safe. Most people in my white, middle-class, North American world did not get shot at. Even adding the fact of my being a lesbian in no way prepared me for murder. Lesbians I knew got called names—an aggravating, uncomfortable, infuriating experience, but not generally dangerous. I grew up as a Jew, knowing that my father had fled from Austria because of the Holocaust. That kind of life-endangering oppression was history to me, or something that happened to other people, with other skin colors or names different from mine.

But now that worldview didn't work anymore. Under the surface of my conscious mind, *Someone like me can't get shot* dissolved and was replaced with an opposite truth, *Someone could murder me*. As a lesbian, as a Jew, as a woman—I was vulnerable. My sense of safety was irreparably shattered. But accepting that vulnerability was better than keeping the shooting as an "abnormal" occurrence, not a possible part of my everyday world. To heal, I had to acknowledge the world as a place that includes the possibility of getting shot and killed at any moment.

What kept me sane through this inevitable conclusion was that I was not alone in it. Anne, Jill, Gina, Satya, Karen, Kevin, and dozens of other people affirmed that, *Yes, that is the world we all live in.* Many of them, particularly my close friends, were also struggling with these realizations. For the first time, we were dealing with assault, murder, guns, homophobia, misogyny close in—that they exist, sometimes in deadly forms. That we are all threatened by them. That being threatened, however, does not have to mean being hobbled. It means paying attention to the threat.

It was as I began to accept that my fear, my sense of helplessness and loss of control were truths I needed to live with, that my worldview radically shifted. I began thinking about antigay violence as a systemic problem, not only my personal trauma. Kevin and Urvashi Vaid at NGLTF were instrumental in teaching me about antigay violence on a national level. Other people were politicized by the case as well. In Ithaca, women formed the Coalition Against Violence to help ensure that the coverage of the case would highlight the struggles of gays and lesbians, and that the press worked to educate the public about antigay violence.

My family, the wider community, and the legal system recognized my trauma and called it what it was: murder, shooting, homophobia, terrorization. There was no confusion of terms, no euphemisms. It was not an "accident," an "unfortunate mistake." We had been hunted and gunned down because of who we were. Unlike survivors of trauma whose circumstances are treated more ambiguously—for example, the Vietnam vets who came home and were celebrated by some, vilified by others—I was a hero in Ithaca. This unified support helped restore my sense of order in the world.

Still, it is an extraordinary thing to have been shot five times and survive. When I was outside our home, I had the sensation of being on exhibit. I could feel their questions: *Will she*

be okay? Will she ever have a lover again? Where are her scars?
Sometimes I was more comfortable discussing antigay violence with a heterosexual, white, male state police officer than
with lesbians from Ithaca whom I had seen around town for
over a decade. Denny could talk about the shooting without
stuttering, and he could say Rebecca's name. Women I knew
much better treated me as though I was fragile. And I *was* fragile, but I wanted to be normal. I wanted to flirt with a woman at
the annual gay and lesbian picnic. I wanted to get a real response
in conversations about other people's work or families.

Even those who were able to cope were very delicate with
me. Approaching mourners is often a double bind: If you pay
attention to my grieving, you've invaded my space, and I'm angry. If you don't pay attention to my grieving, you've ignored a
huge piece of me, and I'm angry. Anne was, perhaps, the only
person who did not show me unquestioning deference. She was
able to respect my healing process without compromising herself, pointing out simple realities about my behavior, especially
around my need to control.

That summer, I craved the return of my independence, to
be able to go where I wanted, when I wanted, without depend-
ing on other people. Though I got slowly better, better meant
having tiny clips of each day when I was not actively processing
the shooting. Even during those few minutes of relief, the feelings of fragility did not leave.

➤

Rebecca and I never broke up—she was just gone. I stared
for hours at the few photographs I had of her, finding her per-
sonality captured in the way she held her body, a smile, or a
cowlick. I was in love with her, like a hose filling up a bucket,
and suddenly the bucket disappeared. The love kept pouring
out of me, spilling on the ground. I was in the untenable position of being in love with someone who was dead. I had to

break up with her alone.

In August, Anne and Gina drove down with me to Blacksburg. Evelyn had hardly touched Rebecca's room since her death. She was dreading the task of cleaning it and sorting through her sister's possessions. So were I and Judy, who had also come for the weekend. I never would have guessed that we would spend the whole day together, laughing at each other as we tried on Rebecca's too-small clothing. We divided up her possessions, roaring and crying at our possessive feelings for each earring or sweater.

We wished there were more photographs of her. I wanted a photograph that showed her sleeping, and waking, and brushing her teeth, and cooking dinner, and working, and kissing me, and gardening. I wanted her alive.

In September, Evelyn moved from the apartment she and Rebecca had shared. I fell into a part-time job. An architect friend knew another architect who was looking for a drafter. I felt ready to work and took the job. My boss knew who "Claudia Brenner" was from the papers, and it seemed okay with him. Phone calls came in to the office, and I would interrupt my drawing of stairs, or a roof plan, to discuss the case with Kevin or Abbe.

I still hadn't finished my Master's degree. I called my committee chair at Virginia Tech and told her I wasn't coming back to school. She was worried that I had lost all my ambition, but ambition was not the problem. I couldn't leave my family and Ithaca for Blacksburg. The best thing she did for me was to be unwilling to compromise the full requirements for my degree. I only had one course and my thesis project left. My chair was flexible and compassionate enough to agree that I could take my last class requirement in the architecture school at Cornell and complete my thesis over the year.

>

On September 19, Roy argued the "no grounds for provocation" brief at a hearing. Michael George's new contention was that he should be able to present personal history as part of the provocation defense. Carr had been abused as a child, both physically and sexually. He had been ridiculed at school while growing up and rejected by women his whole life. In prison, he had been raped by another man. While Michael George had previously asserted that the sight of lesbian lovemaking was enough to cause *anybody* to be homicidal, now he wished to plead a special case for his client's actions based on Carr's personal history. The lawyer requested more time for a formal presentation. This delayed the process, and Judge Spicer did not make a ruling on the defense's motion for over a month.

' SEVEN '

A few weeks before jury selection was to begin, in the early fall, I met Abbe for a preparatory session at her office at CUNY Law School in Queens. She had moved to New York to take a teaching job. She outlined what would happen in court, then strolled around her office asking me unsettling questions, acting out the part of Michael George. But we didn't spend a whole lot of time doing that because she didn't want me to sound rehearsed. She and Roy were pretty pleased with my demeanor as a witness already. We had a discussion about the merits of my parents coming (they would, since lesbians have families—parents, siblings, and children—as well as lovers and friends) and debated what I was going to wear (dressy work clothes, the soft butch look).

We had no other strategy except the absolute truth. Abbe and Roy both felt that the simple facts themselves would be highly compelling for a jury, even for twelve persons suffering from varying degrees of homophobia. Keep the focus on the crimes, not our sexuality. The jury, despite knowing that I was a lesbian, was much more likely to identify with my pain and fear as a victim than with violence perpetrated by a repulsive loser who had been convicted of other crimes and who had lots of evidence against him, including a confession.

On October 24, Judge Spicer realized that a ruling had never been entered on Michael George's requests that my and Rebecca's sexual histories be admitted as evidence. On October 25, Judge Spicer found that the defense could bring up as evidence only the sexual activity that happened the day of the shooting, and only as background explanation. There was still no formal ruling on whether or not the new "evidence" of Stephen Roy Carr's background would make provocation a workable defense, but given the judge's responses thus far, we seemed to have the court on our side.

Perhaps the defense's offer should, therefore, have come as no surprise. My house was contacted by Roy Keefer's office the Wednesday before the Monday jury selection was to begin. I was studying in the Fine Arts Library at Cornell for my Professional Practice course. I called home from the basement pay phone and was told that Michael George had contacted Roy Keefer with a settlement offer, and that Roy had said I was to get back to him immediately.

A long-distance call to Gettysburg was followed by hasty arrangements for everyone to meet there Thursday afternoon so that Roy could outline the proposal to all of us at once. I, Abbe, and Leon Wight could make it the next afternoon, as well as Denny, Don, Matt O'Brien, and John Holtz. I also called Nancie and asked her to come. Judy Wight was going to accompany her father to the meeting. Evelyn was out of town.

Technically, the decision about whether to accept a negotiated settlement belonged solely to the district attorney. Roy was committed, however, to both the families and the police officers who had worked on the case. He wanted to reach a decision we all supported.

By this time, unexpected long-distance trips were becoming commonplace for me; I drove down with Ruth in a borrowed car the next day, and we checked into the now-familiar motel in Gettysburg. The meeting took place at 1:00 P.M. in Roy's of-

fice on an upper floor of the small-town courthouse. This time—
unlike the meeting following the line-up four months earlier,
which took place in the conference room across the hall—we
all gathered into Roy's office, sitting in chairs arranged circu-
larly around the room. There were more of us at this meeting,
not fewer, but now we didn't mind the crowding. I sat next to
Abbe, on the right side of Roy's large wooden desk, and looked
around at the faces I never would have expected to come to
know so well.

Roy outlined the proposal he had received from Michael
George. On behalf of his client, he offered to accept a conviction of first-degree murder, and a sentence of life with no possibility of parole, in return for which we would withdraw our
request for the death penalty and not pursue convictions on the
other charges. This included the charge of attempted murder
on my life.

The offer meant that Michael George saw he had nothing.
Pretrial verdicts all but ruled out "homosexual panic." Stephen
Roy Carr's actions were too deliberate for an insanity plea or a
less-than-first-degree murder charge: He told John Gulden that
he had done a bad thing. He shot a single-bolt action rifle eight
times, reloading shells while Rebecca and I screamed. He ran
and hid. He cried when the police told him that I was alive.
Michael George had not disclosed the results of psychological
testing, but it seemed they had not helped him formulate a defense. Carr's contradictory confession eliminated simply dis-
proving that he had done it, or convincing the jury that it was
an accident.

A complex but orderly discussion ensued among the twelve
of us. What was the likelihood of a first-degree murder conviction from a jury? What about a third-degree conviction, on which
he could get a sentence of ten to twenty years and be eligible for
parole in as little as seven years? What if he were convicted of
third-degree murder plus other charges? What if the jury empa-

thized with Stephen Roy Carr? If they did convict him of first-degree murder, what was the likelihood of getting the death penalty sentencing? What was the likelihood of life without parole—exactly what we were being offered? What did it mean to me to have the charges against Carr stemming from the attack on me be dropped? Could he still appeal? Did life with no parole in Pennsylvania really mean those prisoners did not get released? Did the death penalty in Pennsylvania mean the recipient really got put to death, or did they sit on death row forever?

The four police officers shared their experiences with jury trials, talking about how "squirrely" juries can be: You can think you have a strong conviction locked up, and then a jury will come back with a verdict that convinces you you must have been in different courtrooms. In their collective time on the force, which added up to something like one hundred years, they had often been frustrated by seeing criminals let off, or receive sentences much too light for the wrong perpetrated. This offer was good, and the police all thought we should accept.

On the other hand, there was a sense in the room of *We got 'em*. Roy said that Michael George had only last week listened to the tape Denny and Don had made when I came out to them in the hospital and told them the full story from beginning to end. Roy believed that that tape had shaken Michael George. His offer of a settlement was at least partially motivated by the fact that there were no inconsistencies in my story, in all the tellings—from the tape until the discovery hearing. My accounts did not offer any small openings to grab hold of and tear wider. Roy also thought that hearing me tell the story in its unedited potency scared Michael George. Perhaps he feared the jury would go all the way, convicting his client of first-degree murder and sentencing him to death—a defense attorney's nightmare. In any case, if we decided that we wanted to go to trial, Roy was willing.

I didn't know what to think, and mostly listened during that ninety minutes of earnest discussion. Abbe supported my mixed-up first responses, reminding us all that either decision—trial or settlement—had merit.

Leon Wight, on the other hand, felt that there was only one right thing to do. He was distraught at the notion of a negotiated settlement. Any sentence less than death was unthinkable, and he did not want to even consider the offer.

We needed more time to think, to talk. Roy said he had to let the defense know our decision by the morning, and reemphasized that he was behind whatever choice we made. Then we all left. It was mid-afternoon. Abbe, Leon Wight, and I walked to a restaurant not far from the courthouse.

I had only met Rebecca's father once before, the day of the discovery hearing, but here I was about to discuss the fate of the man who had murdered his daughter. I was nervous about how the conversation would go. Abbe and I ordered coffee. The restaurant around us was tourist-elegant and darkish. Next to me, Mr. Wight denounced a criminal justice system that would feed and clothe and entertain the man who had killed his daughter. They had color TVs in prison. They could take art classes, he pointed out.

It was hard for me to try to get my dead lover's father to see the defense's settlement offer as a reasonable option when I had not yet talked out my issues about it. Mr. Wight left some hours later for his home in D.C., promising to talk with his wife and call us in the morning.

Then Abbe and I went back to the motel where Nancie and Ruth were waiting, and my work began. Sorting through rational and irrational, feelings, thoughts, fears. What were we hoping for? A very substantial offer had been made. First-degree murder with life is a conviction of the highest order, and to have that to work up from was no small thing. In Pennsylvania, Roy had told us, life is life: There is no possibility for parole.

Life convicts only get out on extraordinarily rare pardons from the governor.

On the other hand, there was every reason to believe that a jury would understand the deliberate and intentional nature of Stephen Roy Carr's actions and empathize with me. In fact, Roy had said that a jury would "fall in love with me." It was very conceivable that they would convict Carr of first-degree murder and pronounce the most severe sentence—death.

But what if we turned down first-degree with life, went through all the effort and pain of a trial, and then something went wrong? We had no idea how a jury would really behave, as the police had reminded us. How much could homophobia influence the jury's collective mind? How could I live with a third-degree murder conviction if I had been offered first-degree in settlement and turned it down?

There was a minor concern that the categorization of "capital" offense would not stick. Stephen Roy Carr did not succeed in committing "multiple murder." And his crime may not have fit the definition of "endangering one person's life in the act of killing another" since he had intended to kill us both. Both of those offenses are punishable by death in the state of Pennsylvania, but legal gymnastics could put him in a judicial grey area. Common sense said that the crime fit under and between both categories, but the law is not known for its wisdom, only its logic. This technicality could leave us with a maximum penalty of life without parole, which was where we were starting.

Sixty people were due to show up at the courthouse at 9:00 A.M. on Monday for jury selection. Abbe had begun to review their questionnaires, and I, too, had glanced through the one-and-a-half inch stack of papers. Each sheet seemed oppressively one-dimensional. They were all "capital jurors," jurors who did not in principle object to the death penalty. But how could we even begin to know these people's complex political and cultural values? Could studying an individual's age, education, and occupation tell us anything about whether they would really sentence someone to death? Or whether they had irrational prejudices against lesbianism?

It was frightening that twelve of these strangers would have the power to decide on the appropriate punishment for the murder of Rebecca. The massive leap of faith needed to assume that a jury of almost randomly selected citizens would produce fairness and impartiality was one I was not sure I wanted to make, especially in view of another available option.

Abbe's assessment of the jury pool from Adams County was that we would probably end up with a working-class group, a jury which, statistically, was likely to feel comfortable with the death penalty, but much less likely to feel comfortable with my lesbianism. Even with such a compelling story on our side, the conflicting needs of finding people who were pro-death penalty but not too homophobic were going to make it difficult to select jurors. It was very possible that one individual on the jury would consider Stephen Roy Carr's age a mitigating factor, or see some remorse in him, or understand his motivation to kill lesbians. Any one dissenter on the twelve-person panel would mean that the sentence of life with no parole would be chosen, because the death penalty requires a unanimous decision.

If we were to settle, how would I feel about dropping the charges pertaining to Stephen Roy Carr's attempt on my life? Abbe gave me lots of room to consider this. From a pragmatic point of view, the concern was purely symbolic: The negotiated settlement stipulated that if an appeal was later granted and the case tried, *all* original charges would be reactivated, as well as the request for the death penalty.

It seemed clear that Michael George was going to appeal since Stephen Roy Carr was not pleading guilty. He was simply accepting the conviction of first-degree murder as a settlement. By law, Carr would not be considered guilty. A negotiated settlement meant the defense's appeals would be limited to the court's decisions on pretrial motions. This was good. A jury trial would allow the defense to appeal all rulings, pretrial and trial, thereby providing far more opportunity for legal maneuvering on their part.

Around and around and around. Probabilities and uncertainties. It grew very significant to me that if we chose a jury trial, we were choosing it *after* refusing this offer. That meant we were looking for the death penalty, or the symbolism of the death penalty, its seriousness. In fact, no one had actually been put to death in Pennsylvania in thirty-one years. So we could go through the whole ordeal of a trial only to have Carr sit on death row in the same way that he would sit in prison with a life sentence. But did the pronouncement of Guilty by a jury matter to me?

I spoke again with Rebecca's dad, who continued to have major reservations, and with my parents and family in Ithaca. By late evening, I was certain that accepting the offer made sense. The outcome of a jury trial would very probably be similar to this offer, only more painful to achieve. Abbe was pleased, both because of her strong convictions against the death penalty and because she was quite familiar with the jury process. That night, the decision lay fairly easy with me. I knew that Leon Wight would not likely convince either me or Roy Keefer that it was an error. We would proceed with an adjudicated trial. It was a good decision.

Nancie, Abbe, and I went to the D.A.'s office in the morning. Leon Wight had called Roy. For him, death was the only satisfactory resolution. His oldest daughter had been viciously, senselessly murdered. He wanted revenge. He did not want to settle, but the decision was not up to him alone. The majority wanted to proceed with the settlement, and he was willing, although reluctantly, to accept this outcome.

I believed it was the wisest choice. The system would have so much more leeway to demonstrate its ineptitude—the more you relied on it, the more likely it was to screw up—if we went to trial.

Roy scheduled an "adjudicated trial" for that afternoon at one o'clock. Leon and Judy Wight were on the road back to Gettysburg from D.C. to be present at it.

›

The motions of the adjudicated trial were all prestaged, but the tension was still very high. Would it really come off as planned?

Abbe and I entered the courtroom and sat right near the rail. The expected cast of characters were present: many people from my life and Rebecca's, the police officers, reporters. The middle section of seats, to our right, was filled by the media. I felt watched, and, in fact, I *was* being watched. This was still a big case locally and for the national gay press.

Abbe's presence next to me made me feel secure. I trusted her and believed she would not forget what was important to me, personally and politically. Throughout the case, I had faith in her judgment about the legal system and the full breadth of her knowledge of criminal law. We were very fortunate that Roy also saw Abbe as an ally, including her fully in the decision-making process.

A very different scenario could have played out if the district attorney felt threatened by additional counsel. Perhaps he would not have postponed the discovery hearing. Perhaps the provocation motion would not have been filed. Perhaps Michael George would not have felt as cornered and we would have had to go to trial. Or I might not have felt as secure and cared for, which would have taken its emotional toll and perhaps been reflected in my testimony and judgment. As it was, the personalities involved meshed beautifully.

Roy Keefer was at the prosecution table. Stephen Roy Carr, who had been brought in by guards shortly after we arrived, now sat, unshackled, next to Michael George. He was horribly vacant and unappealing, as if there was no spirit in him against which to react at all.

Roy spoke first. He outlined for the record the agreed upon stipulations. A real indication of the comradeship between Abbe Smith and Roy Keefer occurred at the close of his requests to the judge. Roy turned and walked to the bar separating the audience from the court, leaned to Abbe, and asked, "Did I forget anything?"

Then it was Michael George's turn. It was strange to hear Stephen Roy Carr's defense attorney refer to him as "Steve," or hear him describe anecdotes of Carr's jail time thus far—that he did artwork, that he had had a conversation with the barber—because any personhood was so radically absent from Stephen Roy Carr's presence. I found it hard to reconcile his violent actions with the fact that he was a human being. His appearance did little to humanize him. I hated him, and with no hesitation would have traded his life for Rebecca's. But my prevailing feeling was of a void, as if his own lack of substance nullified even hatred directed at it. I felt a barren loathing throughout the tense proceedings, and the feeling has never left me.

At this point, Michael George made a last-ditch attempt.

"Your Honor," he said, "before agreeing to any stipulations, there is presently pending before the court an issue on whether or not provocation is a viable defense in this situation. I am going to ask the court to resolve that issue prior to making any agreement and offer proof as to the relevancy of a provocation defense.

"We are prepared to present testimony that Stephen Carr has been sexually abused as he was growing up by a neighbor of his. We are willing to present evidence that Stephen Carr has been sexually abused by a male in the prison system down in Florida. We are prepared to present evidence that Stephen Carr's mother may be involved in a lesbian relationship. We are willing to present evidence that Stephen Carr has, because of his lifestyle in growing up, been ridiculed through the school system.

"We are prepared to present testimony that every attempt he ever had to carry on a relationship with a woman has been refused and in effect has resulted in him being termed a freak or similar adjectives.

"We are prepared to present evidence that what happened on the afternoon of May 13, 1988 affected Steve's ability and pushed him," and here Michael George began to repeat himself, "ability to reason, and pushed him over the edge and provoked him, in effect, to doing the act which he is alleged of doing should the court find that is what occurred."

Judge Spicer asked if he was correct in understanding that Michael George was asking the court to make a ruling on the spot.

The defense attorney agreed, adding, "One fact which I do want the court to take into consideration is that the women were engaged in a lesbian act at the time the incident occurred."

"All right," said Judge Spicer. "That's the offer upon which you wish the ruling made?"

"Yes, it is, Your Honor."

Then the judge ruled that sexual conduct of any kind, for any reason, in the context of this case, could not be considered legal provocation.

He spoke at length to Stephen Roy Carr to ensure that he understood the settlement offer and was entering the agreement "freely."

"Do you waive your right to a trial by a jury of your peers?" "Do you know that accepting the verdict of this trial will mean that you will spend the rest of your life in prison?" "Are you aware that you will never be eligible for parole?"

It was nerve-wracking for me to hear the repetitive questioning. I imagined Stephen Roy Carr impulsively, or with a sudden new awareness, withdrawing his acceptance. We remained poised for anything.

When Stephen Roy Carr responded to the judge, it was bizarre for me to actually hear his voice. The only words I had ever heard him say were "Are you lost already?" and "See you later." Answering one question at a time, he spoke the expected phrases, agreeing first to waive his right to a full jury trial and accept the adjudicated trial, and so on and so on. His voice was leaden. He would not have made an impressive defendant before a jury.

The judge finally had Stephen Roy Carr say that he accepted the conviction of first-degree murder with a sentence of life imprisonment. Very quickly the proceedings were closed. Of course, postverdict motions for appeal were going to be filed by Michael George. Stephen Roy Carr was led away. We sat for a moment. Abbe squeezed my arm. There were quiet hugs as we filed out of the courtroom. If Rebecca had lived, everyone would have been hugging her too. She and I would have been hugging each other.

Before the sentencing, Abbe had helped me prepare a statement which I read at a press conference afterward.

"My name is Claudia Brenner," I began. I was just barely able to read correctly. To myself, my words sounded hollow and my voice distant. I hadn't had any time to come down from the court proceedings, and this was the first occasion on which I spoke directly to the media. Had the words not been prewritten, I don't think I could have been coherent.

"It seems to me that a life sentence with no parole in a maximum security prison, while not compensating for our tremendous loss and pain, is the appropriate response to a nightmare that nothing can ever make right.

"Rebecca and I were lovers. As the judge ruled, nothing about who we were or our love for each other could be considered motivation for the outrageous, inhumane violence that Stephen Roy Carr perpetrated against us. While I am angry that the notion of provocation could even surface in this case—that someone could suggest that who we were and what we were doing could reasonably prompt someone to kill us—I am glad that the law is clear that there was no provocation.

"I am also heartened by the respectful and professional manner in which the case was handled by the Pennsylvania state police and the Adams County district attorney's office. All those involved never wavered in the investigation and prosecution of this serious crime. In particular, I want to thank State Trooper Denny Beaver for his warmth and kindness throughout this ordeal.

"I am fortunate to have worked with such an incredible team of people. Most gay people who are victims of violence do not receive the kind of treatment that I received—that any person who's been the victim of crime deserves. The ignorance and bigotry that underlies the violence here, and the violence which lesbians and gay men experience every day, is pervasive in our society.

"Rebecca's tragic death and my own near-death are deeply felt by many—both those who knew her, and those who knew her only through her death. I have been deeply touched by everyone's response.

"I can't begin to express our collective grief, and how much we miss her."

There were just a few questions asked of me, as well as Abbe, Roy, and the police. Mostly, the press seemed satisfied with the prepared statement and went off to file their stories. Had it not been for Abbe's foresight, I might have been another victim trounced on by journalists to capture the emotion to which the media feels they are entitled.

Abbe had advised me early on not to talk to the media until the case was over because she did not want us to unintentionally reveal anything to the defense. That seclusion also gave me the privacy I needed to do emotional healing over the months leading up to the court decision. I got to handle the media on my own terms.

After it was all over, Abbe, Ruth, and I joined our police officers and Roy at a tavern on the way out of town. It was an impromptu debriefing and celebration. We laughed and ate the cherry pie that Denny brought from a special bakery he had frequented during the case, on his constant commutes between Harrisburg and Gettysburg. We had reason to celebrate. The system had worked. The right person had received the right conviction. If only Rebecca had not died.

Denny and Don were genuinely puzzled by my feeling "heartened" by their "respectful and professional manner" and "fortunate to have worked with such an incredible team." Weren't they just being human? Why is justice for a lesbian or gay victim such a laudable achievement, they asked us.

On the one hand, we explained, of course they were just being human. Any officer should have been respectful of me and compassionate about Rebecca's death. At the same time, it was incredible that they had been able to leap over their stereotypes and cultural training to treat me just like a heterosexual victim, and her death like the death of any straight person's partner.

Maybe, we hypothesized, their vast underestimation of the small miracle that had occurred came from believing, falsely, that we were "exceptional" lesbians.

The police most often deal with two kinds of people: victims and perpetrators. These individuals do not represent a random sampling of the population, gay or straight. Ruth, Abbe, and I tried to shed light, for Denny and Don, on two of the fundamental pillars of homophobia: the "heterosexual assumption" and the "all gays are alike" myth.

The police frequently see victims of routine crimes: property trespassed, a car stolen, a home burglarized. A woman calling to complain about her raucous neighbors rarely chooses to reveal her sexual orientation, and she is particularly unlikely to do so if she believes she will be discriminated against for saying she is a lesbian. The average perpetrator of a petty offense, such as speeding or vandalism, will likewise not usually disclose personal details of his or her life. This omission tends to perpetuate the myth that all people are heterosexual.

Then there are the criminals. When a gay or lesbian detainee does come out to the police, her situation is different by definition from the "average" gay person. Most gay people, like most straight people, are not criminals. If someone is involved in a crime, they may very well also be having other problems. Troubles with drugs or money or family often are a backdrop for illegal or antisocial actions. The gay or lesbian criminal does not present an accurate slice of gay and lesbian life to a police officer. So, if everyone is straight except for some serious offenders, and an officer does not have an out family member, friend, or coworker, he or she will not see lesbians and gay men in their full diversity. Only as stereotypes.

Denny told us that the only out lesbians he had encountered before us were two women having a drunken domestic dispute, wielding broken bottles. He had never met a lesbian graduate student studying architecture with strong family and community ties.

Antihomophobia training might have helped him have different images of lesbians and gays, but this case was far more powerful an influence. I was more than just a statistic or a tragedy read about in the paper. Denny and Don got to know me and my family really well. It is true, as the studies indicate, that personal experience most effectively transforms homophobic prejudice. Denny admitted that his perspective toward lesbians had changed over time as he grew to know and care about us.

He and Don also acknowledged that the shift might not have come as easily had the victims of Stephen Roy Carr's bullets been two gay men. We knew that this would have been a whole different story, because gay men threaten straight men's notions of what it is to be a man, whereas Denny and Don didn't have to identify with me and my family in order to sympathize with us.

By the time we had finished our pie and beer, they were less baffled but still amazed by the degree of homophobia we expected from the system and them. Denny and Don continued to disavow the praise they got, believing that they were just being decent.

꘏

The appeals began. I started on my thesis project and continued to work as a drafter. Gina got more pregnant. Leaves in the gorges of Ithaca changed colors, then they dropped to the ground, to become covered with snow. Taylor Thomas Warren Kolb was born. The snow melted. The appeals process continued.

Years before May 13, 1988, Stephen Roy Carr had been robbing elderly people in retirement communities. He was apprehended after stabbing a victim. (He claimed to the police that the eighty-year-old woman he was robbing lunged at him, impaling herself on the knife he held motionless.) After serving prison time, Carr got out on parole and fled the state illegally. It was the "fugitive from justice" warrant from the state of Florida that the Pennsylvania state police used to arrest him.

From Abbe's "defense attorney perspective," the initial decision not to accuse Stephen Roy Carr of murder posed the only substantial issue for postverdict appeal. Either caution or strategy made the police question him first regarding the fugitive warrant. They waited several hours to say explicitly, "You are being charged with murder."

While the law gives the police some latitude to interrogate as they see best, a suspect must nevertheless know for what crime he is being questioned. Stephen Roy Carr said a lot of things in those first few hours. He agreed, for example, to take them to the gun. The gun, therefore, would probably be disallowed in an appealed case. This would damage the case but not destroy it.

There was ample evidence besides the gun, all pointing unmistakably to Carr. In order to get a new proceeding, the defense had to prove that the change in evidence could alter the outcome of the case. It would not be enough that slightly different lines of argument might be made in the trial. The judge would need to have reason to believe that the ultimate outcome, Stephen Roy Carr's conviction of first-degree murder and the impending sentence of life imprisonment, would be reduced or reversed.

On April 3, 1989, Judge Oscar Spicer wrote an Order of the Court of Common Pleas on Michael George's four postverdict motions.

The first motion was about the validity of Stephen Roy Carr's confession and the evidence of the gun, based on the initial execution of the fugitive warrant rather than a murder warrant. Judge Spicer overruled that motion, saying that it was obvious from his responses to the police that Carr knew the questions being asked were about more than the fugitive from justice charge, and that Carr waived his Miranda rights even so.

The second motion concerned not having the coroner— the "expert witness"—available at the pretrial discovery. Judge Spicer overruled this motion, stating that it was obvious that demands on the coroner's time explained his absence.

The third motion concerning "pretrial requests for disclosure," which meant that Michael George wanted the fact that Rebecca and I were lesbians to be admissible in court, was likewise disallowed. Judge Spicer had already ruled, based on the earlier argument made by Roy and Abbe, that "such information was irrelevant to the charges." He now added, "The victims' actions and/or inclinations prior to the fatal shots cannot be made relevant by any analysis."

Finally, Judge Spicer addressed the defense's argument that

"he was entitled to present evidence to reduce murder to man-slaughter" because Stephen Roy Carr was provoked. Michael George claimed that his client went to the woods to escape the "evils of the world," i.e., lesbianism, sex, and women. Judge Spicer wrote:

> Defendant's motives in taking to the wilderness are subject to debate. He was, after all, a fugitive from justice. However, it may be true, as Defendant's counsel suggests, he chose a primeval setting to escape the evils of the world. At the first glance of what he contends was evil, however, he eagerly pursued it for a better view.
>
> We think the evidence suggests that the two women were the ones attempting to escape. They sought the solitude of a location thought pristine. Many may frown upon what they did, but they broke no law and only pursued activities in which they had a right to engage.
>
> Defendant, on the other hand, brought an attitude and disposition that would be considered evil in any civilized circumstance.
>
> People seem to live constantly in eras when one group or another feel justified in ending human life for reasons thought to be sufficient. History is replete with examples of utmost cruelty being inflicted upon those termed heretic, witches, sodomites and the like. We have recently seen a religious leader in one country issue a death sentence because of something authored in another country.
>
> If there was no law, there would be an impressive list of words and deeds that would minimize the seriousness of taking of life by someone offended or stimulated...[The Defendant's] murderous act cannot be mitigated by such trivial provocation.

The judge summarized: "...a person who intentionally kills a stranger should not be able to expect lessened punishment because of revulsion or disapproval of the victim's conduct."

,

Six weeks after Judge Spicer's decision, on May 17, 1989, we all appeared in court again for the sentencing proceeding. A year had passed since the shooting. Taylor, at three months, was the youngest spectator in the courtroom. Evelyn and Judy Wight were there, along with their parents. Anne, Gina, Ruth, and other friends from Ithaca and Blacksburg attended too.

Both Leon Wight and I read Victim Impact Statements which became part of the official record, to follow Stephen Roy Carr to any further appeals or clemency proceedings.

"I wish I did not have to make this statement," I began. "I wish that my experiences in Adams County, Pennsylvania had ended, as planned, on May 15, 1988. I wish that Rebecca and I were making plans for where we wanted to hike and backpack this summer. I wish that the inconceivable pain and horror I experienced were fears with no basis in reality, that the sound of shots, that shattering reality in my mind, was a bad dream from which I could awaken."

I described watching Rebecca struggling, dying. I told the court how my unhealed body and heart were daily reminders of loss—of my lover, my sense of safety, my privacy.

"I wish that Mr. Michael George had found a way of defending his client that did not attempt to blame the victims, that did not add sensationalism for the media to exploit, that did not augment the pain I had already endured through the vicious and murderous actions of his client.

"At one level, I am furious. I am outraged that Stephen Roy Carr, for whatever savage personal reasons, violently imposed his will on my life. I am angry that our victimization could be portrayed by the defense attorney in inflammatory and distorted terms, and that he would attempt to exploit the fact that we had a lesbian relationship.

"My life has been altered irreparably and I know I will always be inconsolable about Rebecca's death and a future I will never have with her. It is through tremendous effort, remarkable support and assistance, that I can speak as a healthy individual today. I did not heal by myself. I healed and continue to heal because people helped me. From the moment I found help on Shippensburg Road after walking out of the woods, I got the best help I could imagine: emergency medical, police, legal, and personal.... Not only my friends but also people who barely knew me and strangers who did not know me at all responded with warmth and also with outrage. It is only because of these responses that I have managed to heal. The only antidote to the horror of the shooting has been the incredible kindness that I have received since that time and the realization of the appropriate conclusion to the court proceedings."

It was clear from Leon Wight's Victim Impact Statement that he was still deeply disturbed by Stephen Roy Carr being alive—able to watch TV in prison or breathe fresh air—while his daughter was dead. I was less troubled by this. Years before, when I had worked with delinquent adolescents, we used to take them to a maximum security prison for a "Scared Straight" equivalent. Those experiences convinced me that regardless of any comforts or educational programs available in prison, the conditions behind maximum security bars were horrible.

Stephen Roy Carr was sentenced to life imprisonment with no parole.

As long as there was going to be full, permanent restriction on Carr's access to society, I cared little about his daily existence. I had been told that life without parole carries low status among the inmate population, which probably meant that in prison, he would not be popular. The sentence also meant that he could virtually be forgotten by the Department of Corrections and rot in prison. Death row inmates, on the other hand, sometimes attract right-leaning vigilante groups or left-leaning activists, and the case stays in the public eye.

My only small worry was that Carr would acclimate so well to prison that he would appear a "model prisoner" and apply to the governor for clemency. However, in Pennsylvania pardons are first permitted after seventeen years and rarely granted until a prisoner is close to death. Also, Stephen Roy Carr's gory dossier would follow him to any future request for clemency. And finally, the possibility of clemency was too far in the future and too uncontrollable to let it absorb much of my mental energy.

My thinking about the death penalty as court proceedings approached was nothing like the intellectualizing about it I had done in the past, my knowledge of how biased the system is against the poor, or people of color. Stephen Roy Carr's life was worthless. As I walked down the Ithaca Commons, if I could have made the magical substitution of Carr's life for Rebecca's, I would have done it in an instant.

Stephen Roy Carr receiving the death penalty would have meant that the State recognized the lasting consequences of his actions. The problem was that the murderer himself could not be forced to comprehend his wrongdoings—not in prison, not even on the way to a lethal injection. Nothing that could be imposed from the outside could ensure that Stephen Roy Carr would go through such harsh self-reflection. If he were capable of any reflection and repentance at all, I was sure introspection would lead him to take his own life. To me, that might have demonstrated comprehension of the everlasting pain he inflicted. Unfortunately, there was no way for the State to work that kind of transformation.

· EIGHT ·

T hree weeks after the sentencing, June 7, 1989, I am standing next to Kevin Berrill in Washington, D.C., Dirkson Senate Office Building. An NGLTF press conference: "Anti-Gay Violence, Victimization and Defamation in 1988."

We're in an enormous carpeted room with a high ceiling and large windows. Cushioned banquet chairs filled with reporters, perhaps one hundred of them. Television cameras and lights banked against the rear wall. The talking and folding over of pads of paper rustle like the beginning of an exam.

Representative John Conyers, progressive Michigan Democrat, House sponsor of the Federal Hate Crimes Statistics Act, introduces the report from behind the podium of fine wood with the seal of the United States Congress. Tape recorders click on.

Kevin: "Today's report is our annual wake-up call. It is our reminder to the nation that the price of antigay bigotry is paid in human lives lost and in immeasurable suffering for the victims, their loved ones, and our entire community." He gives statistics from the 1988 NGLTF report on antigay violence nationally. Eighty percent of lesbians, gays, and bisexuals have been verbally abused. Nineteen percent have had their property vandalized. Forty-four percent of us have been threatened with violence. Seventeen percent have actually experienced a physical assault. Nine percent have been assaulted with a weapon.

I hear Kevin's voice but none of the words. I'm thinking about going next. Suddenly, I am in front of the podium.

I have a prepared statement in front of me. Urvashi Vaid, Public Information Director of the Task Force, edited my comments the day before and prepared them for the press packet. That was my first face to face meeting with anyone from NGLTF, although I had talked to Kevin and others many times on the phone. They had been coming through for me consistently since last May.

"Statistics about murder, death, and tragedy mean different things to me now," I begin. My role is to be me. I did not quite expect this much media. I had never envisioned what a national press conference in the U.S. Senate would be like.

"No longer can a death be impersonal. For me, each death now comes with a face, and my heart cries with the loss of a loved one. When death comes intentionally, it is harder to bear. We find ways of incorporating accidents into our moral fabric, though we still suffer from those losses. But the horror of intentional, unprovoked murder 'threatens to extinguish the warmth of the human soul.'"*

It amazes me that my reactions and feelings about the shooting can transform and slide into words.

"It comes with pain and suffering and loss. It comes with a broken heart. It comes with images that still bring tears as I think them. It comes with nightmares. It comes with anger and the incredible frustration of absolute injustice. And it stays. It's possible to go forward with life, but the sadness and loss stay.

"Rebecca was murdered. Sometimes, still, these words, spoken or written, are absolutely unbelievable. How could that be true? I was just with her. We were hiking, eating oranges, chatting about the future and the past. Smiling in the sunshine

*Judy Barringer, *One Day in Ithaca: May 17, 1988,* edited by Carol Kammen (Ithaca, Centennial Press, 1989), p. 192.

of May. Loving each other and the outdoors. Wasn't she just there beside me?

"One time, Rebecca and I were together near Niagara Falls. I had been studying abroad and just returned. We were walking in the cold air and she put her arm around me as we walked. I was surprised because Rebecca did not generally feel safe to express her affection in public. She felt safe that day. She said to me, 'We're so happy Claudia, how could anybody hurt us?' as though our happiness could provide a shield against any aggression we might encounter.

"Before May 13, 1988, I believed that we, as lesbians, could be hurt or harassed. With words, most likely; maybe with some force if things got out of hand. I had accepted the potential harassment gay people are accustomed to, the kind of harassments that comprise more than two-thirds of the 1988 report that Kevin Berrill spoke of. Nobody should have to worry about brutal murder. I didn't. I lived my life, chose my love respectfully and honorably, as I believe all people should.

"Brutal attempted murder happened to me. And killed Rebecca. It happened because we were identified as lesbians. By a stranger, with whom we had no connection. The fact that crimes are targeted against particular groups, in this case lesbians, requires a societal response. Part of the response it requires is passage of the kind of legislation Senator Simon and Representative Conyers are sponsoring.

"I was fortunate. First, that I lived. Second, that people really helped. The criminal justice system has responded appropriately to the murderous actions of Stephen Roy Carr. He will spend the rest of his life in prison, with no possibility of parole. But Rebecca, who was twenty-eight years old, is gone. I struggle every day with the arduous process of healing from such unbearable trauma.

"Though I had an extraordinarily good experience with the state police and the district attorney of Adams County, my lesbianism and the nature of the crime committed were of grave concern to me. For three days in the trauma center and intensive care unit of Hershey Medical Center, I did not tell the state police I was a lesbian, that Rebecca and I were lovers, that I knew the shooting was hate-motivated. Because I was terrified. My closest friend, an ex-lover, told the hospital she was my sister. Because we were afraid the system would not embrace us, would not respect the nature of our bonding. Though we managed well in that particular case, we, as victims, need the assurance of knowing the systems will embrace us. No victim should be victimized by fear of the system designed to help.

"I wish that by my being here today, as people reflect upon the statistics of this report, they will be able to add a face and a story to the numbers. And, if to further the goal of humanitarian response to violence against gays and lesbians, we need to compile statistics, then I, as a victim, and as a statistic, stand in support of the proposed Hate Crime Statistics Act."

Following my statement, the questions from the press are factual. They want me to tell them about the shooting.

I can do that. The power of the story drives itself. It streams out into the sea of reporters, from my memory, in my voice.

Had there been time to consider the implications of a national press conference, I might have foreseen the events that followed. The NGLTF report was news. The issue of antigay violence was just floating to the surface of consciousness in the U.S., and the ravenous media pounced on it: Kevin Berrill and Claudia Brenner, Mr. Statistics and the Human Dimension. Before my plane landed in Ithaca, *CBS This Morning* was on the phone to NGLTF requesting our joint appearance in New York.

A uniformed driver greeted me at the Newark Airport baggage claim and ushered me to a waiting luxury car. Kevin and I stayed at a midtown hotel overlooking Central Park. We spent our food allowances eating fabulous Chinese food for dinner and a breakfast of eggs Benedict laid out on china and white table linen.

We were chauffeured to the West Side CBS studio, very early, and found ourselves in a large, high-ceilinged room with sections dividing familiar scenes from *CBS This Morning*. Each setup was no bigger than the view of a camera lens. We were delivered on to a busy set for a live interview.

There were quick brushes with production and make-up people, and a short chat with Harry Reasoner as we settled into the living room facade and were properly miked. We watched the weather segment finish. How do you summarize your experiences in a few short responses? Answer the question and remember to inject your own message. Don't wait. You won't have very much time. Try not to stumble over words. Try not to start a sentence with *Um* or *Well*. Try to look into the camera or at the interviewer. How do I look? It's over before you have time to remember all the reminders. Hustled out of the studio.

Back to the hotel. An enormous amount of effort and money for a few brief moments: national media. Kevin and I celebrated. It was powerful. We managed to convey our message in the short segment. I looked okay. I didn't look at the camera, though. My eyes were down.

Sally Jesse Raphael. Who's she? A talk show with a live audience is a very different thing from a news interview. I learned from Kevin how to question the producers. What's the angle? Is this a "debate" on "the gay lifestyle?" Victims of antigay violence do not have to participate in debates, Kevin counseled. Will the "other side" be represented? There is no debate about violence. They *want* you, Claudia, so make sure that you and your story are treated respectfully. Your story helps break the stereotypes about who we are and who gets attacked.

Long-distance phoning. More phoning, with Sally Jesse Raphael's staff. We finally decided their intentions were honorable. The scheduling was tight—Satya's high school graduation was the same day. They said it was the only time they had. It would probably be fine. Quick planning, and I was on my way to New Haven for the taping.

A white limousine met me at the airport and deposited me at a fancy hotel. I visited with an old friend who lived in the area the night before the taping. At this studio, there was more time before the show than at CBS. Make-up. I met the other panel members in a room laden with food and beverages. Sally Jesse came in to make contact with each of us and review the structure of the segment. She seemed sincere and interested.

Everyone settled into their chairs and was miked. Preprogrammed applause. I was seated next to Sally. There were five of us. Two representatives of high profile antigay murder cases were part of the panel; I'd heard of them through NGLTF. The district attorney from Bucks County, Pennsylvania, who prosecuted the two men who brutally murdered Anthony Milano. A friend of Charlie Howard's, who was writing a book about Howard's tragic death at the hands of homophobic teens in Bangor, Maine. There was also another victim, Mr. Statistics, and me.

By TV standards, I had a significant chunk of time to speak. I was learning how to speak under pressure. Prepare a statement and then expand on it. Answer questions as needed. Sally's questions seemed designed for maximum emotion, but I was there to educate. My answers were good.

The questions from the audience were a bit contrived. The planted adolescents asked if men who carry purses shouldn't expect to be thrown from a bridge. It is important to appear on shows with wide viewing audiences, I reminded myself.

On the trip home there were delays at Newark. The President's entourage came through, tieing up everything. I missed Satya's graduation ceremony. It was awful. I was miserable waiting for the next plane at the airport, kicking myself the whole time for succumbing to the producer's pressure. Talk shows are great exposure for the issues, but I should have said no or insisted that the scheduling meet my needs.

I became practiced at negotiating with producers who had lost track of everything other than their daytime host on a few square inches of TV screen. I got seasoned at distilling the case and frontloading politics. Kevin was a wonderful mentor. Eventually I became able to discern quality interviewing and production from offers of superficial tokenism.

I started to call the commitments "gigs." I had many interviews with the gay press and invitations to speak at conferences and universities. Speaking in front of large groups became a part of my life.

>

In 1990, I spoke at a large demonstration in support of the New York State Hate Crimes Bill. There were over a thousand people milling in front of the monumental concrete steps leading up to the lofty dome of the state capital building in Albany. I stood silently at first, the mike on a stand in front of me.

I had accepted the invitation to speak without thinking too much about it. At a pre-rally candlelight vigil, I realized how many people would be there the next day. That night, and the morning that followed, I struggled to define what experience I was able to give to the rally attendees that they could not get from one of the many other eloquent activists on the program.

I recognized that my message was different from a theoretical lecture on the impact of antigay violence. It was the truth of the personal: I had experienced and survived the violence we all sought to stop. Now I needed to convey the impact of that violence to a huge crowd. No camera would be zooming in for a close-up of my face. How could I communicate the shock and horror of bullets with only words?

When I was shot, there was no time for preparation. No

one said to me, "In five minutes you're going to get shot." I wanted my speech to hit people without warning as well.

Fortuitously, I had a poet in my life, a new lover who lived in Albany. With her help, I crafted a four-page speech entitled "Eight Bullets."

I placed myself close to the microphone. With no introduction, I began:

> The First Bullet: When the first bullet hit me my arm exploded. My brain could not make the connections fast enough to realize I had been shot. I saw a lot of blood on the green tarp on which we lay and thought for a split second about earthquakes and volcanoes. But they don't make you bleed. Rebecca knew. She asked me where I had been shot. We had encountered a stranger earlier that day who had a gun. We both knew who was shooting us. Perhaps a second passed.

> The Second Bullet: When the second bullet hit my neck I started to scream with all my strength. Somehow the second bullet was even more unbelievable than the first.

> The Third Bullet: The third bullet came and I now know hit the other side of my neck. By then I had lost track of what was happening or where we were except that I was in great danger and it was not stopping.

> The Fourth Bullet: I now know a fourth bullet hit me in the face. Rebecca told me to get down, close to the ground.

> The Fifth Bullet: The fifth bullet hit the top of my head. I believe Rebecca saw that even laying flat I was vulnerable, and she told me to run behind a tree.

The Sixth Bullet: The sixth bullet hit Rebecca in the back of her head as she rose to run for the tree.

The Seventh Bullet: The seventh bullet hit Rebecca's back as she ran. It exploded her liver and caused her to die.

The Eighth Bullet: The eighth bullet missed.

It is not surprising that Stephen Roy Carr believed us both dead. He shot to kill. The Neck. The Head. The Back. A single-bolt action rifle that he loaded, shot, and unloaded eight times. Surely he believed us both dead or he would have used more of the twenty-five rounds of ammunition he left in his haste to get away.

He shot from where he was hidden in the woods eighty-five feet away, after he stalked us, hunted us, spied on us. Later his lawyer tried to assert that our sexuality provoked him.

He shot us because he identified us as lesbians. He was a stranger with whom we had no connection.

I am the statistic we speak of when we talk about hate violence. Rebecca is the statistic who is not with us. She is one of the murdered. Murder is a horrible word to incorporate into your day-to-day vocabulary. But it is unfortunately part of the vocabulary of our community. When accidents happen that take a life of a loved one, we find ways of incorporating that loss into our moral fabric, though we suffer. When death comes through the intentional actions of another, it is harder to bear. The horror of intentional unprovoked murder threatens to extinguish the warmth of the human soul.

Statistics, those impersonal numbers we are struggling so hard to collect, are about those murders. They are about real people. They are about me. And Rebecca Wight. And Charlie Howard. And Anthony Milano. And James Zapolarti. And Rod Johnson. And so many other victims on the continuum of antigay violence. Statistics about murder, death, and tragedy are personal to me. Each one has a face and a story, a family, a lover, a life damaged, a grieving process, the pain of loss, and fear, nightmares, images, anger, and the incredible frustration of absolute injustice.

Before May 13, 1988, I believed that we, as lesbians and gay men, could be harassed. With words most likely. Maybe with some force if things got out of hand. I had accepted the potential harassment gay people are accustomed to, the kind of harassment that comprises two-thirds of reported statistics to the National Gay and Lesbian Task Force Anti-Violence Project. The kind we must stop accepting.

I did not consider brutal murder born of hatred and ignorance. Nobody should have to worry about brutal murder. I didn't. I lived my life, chose my love respectfully and honorably as I believe all people should. I thought I was playing by the unwritten rules that would keep me safe. The rules that keep us more hidden than we need to be. The rules that didn't keep me safe. Because brutal attempted murder happened to me. And killed Rebecca. We need to stop following rules that limit us, and act to make the world the place we want it to be. The fact that violence and crimes are targeted against a particular group, in this case gay and lesbian people, requires a societal response. This state government needs to lead that response by passage of the legislation we lobby for today.

Stephen Roy Carr did not succeed in killing me. I survived that day and the months that followed when my life was consumed with pain and loss. I commit myself to not relinquishing any part of my life. For if I let fear take any part of my freedom, Stephen Roy Carr will have succeeded in his goal. We cannot give up any more lives, or parts of our lives, our freedom, or our civil rights, to the forces of violence, whether organized in Far Right hate groups like the one that attacked Rod Johnson, or unorganized actions like the one which killed Rebecca and nearly killed me.

As I'm speaking now, I can feel the lump on the side of my tongue caused by the bullet that shredded my tongue. It is a continual reminder of the shooting, which I feel dozens of times every day. I'm asking you to also be reminded, of your commitment to action, education, and change.

Thank you.

Delivering that speech was a turning point for me. My self-confidence was boosted, and I understood the singular contribution that I had not chosen, but found myself able, to give. In those moments in front of the microphones, I educated the public about antigay violence simply by being myself. There was no separation between the wider world and my personal life.

The personal is powerful. Statistics may be shocking, but they are not raw enough to cut through layers of numbness and resistance. People responded to the scars on my neck. They were scared or outraged; it made them want to do something. The horror that was uniquely mine was given significance through work that was uniquely mine.

I thought about becoming a professional activist. I could have ridden that first wave of interest and kept a steady stream of gigs scheduled. But placing gay activism first would have meant prioritizing a commitment that was not about my self. I was an architect first. My commitment to architecture preceded the shooting. Just as I refused to give up being a lesbian, finishing school, or traveling to new places in response to Stephen Roy Carr's terrorism, I was unwilling to restructure my career path. Nonetheless, I incorporated gay activism into my life.

The feedback I got consistently was that my telling the story made a difference. It expanded images of who victims are. It dispelled stereotypes. Lesbians had not generally been part of the public's picture of victims of gay-bashing. The image was usually of men leaving urban gay bars late at night in a seedy part of town, and getting beat up by some local thugs. Crimes did not take place in rural settings. Crimes were not committed by strangers. Crimes did not result in death.

›

I know my presentations are scary. Whether the listeners are gay or straight, the story of the shooting contains pieces of everyone's worst nightmare. At one of my earlier talks at a college, a young woman spoke. First, she pointed out that she was heterosexual. Then she shared that sometimes when she and her female friends hadn't seen each other for a while, they hugged and kissed in public. What she wanted to know was whether this activity was safe, i.e., would she be mistaken for a lesbian? Could she be shot? At first I was taken aback. Was this a serious question? Then I felt an immense wave of sadness: How tightly confined we all are by established gender roles, and how harsh the punishments by society for pushing the boundaries and stepping outside even the tiniest amount.

That she even asked the question meant she already knew the answer. The violence is not limited to lesbian targets. Victims of antigay violence need only be perceived as lesbians: two straight women friends being physical with each other, a mother and a daughter, a woman single and happy, a woman wearing a tie. To be affectionate with another woman is to be in danger. To be with another woman is to be in danger. To be without a man is to be in danger. To be like a man is to be in danger. Any bending of gender norms is a threat. Women (and men) straying from their designated sex roles are threatened back into them. "Antigay" violence is not limited to gay people.

Audience members will often disclose their own experiences with violence. I have heard about the scars left by violence in many, many people. Too often, the victim has never had a chance to talk about them; it is considered inappropriate in our society to do so. My experience has been that people want to know, want to share, and have their own stories to tell. My sharing often unlocks the gates. To those who have been hurt and those who are scared, I offer the tenet around which I built my personal healing: Deal with the fears. Speak about them. Deal with the past. Retell it. Cry about it. Rage about it. Discuss these issues in a workshop after the talk, with a therapist, or with friends. If we permit fear to paralyze us, than the perpetrator will have succeeded.

My story also contains elements of an exhilarating vision: What if gay men and lesbians, bisexual, transexual, and transgender people were consistently treated with dignity and respected as I was by the criminal justice system.

Once I gave a presentation to the New Haven police department. A young Connecticut state trooper approached me afterward. She expressed surprise at my talk because, as a police officer, she had expected to get "beat up"—guilt-tripped and railed at—and she didn't. She had expected to hear a horror story of lesbian revictimization by the criminal justice system, ineptitude or callousness on the part of police officers, and unsuccessful prosecution by the district attorney's office—and she didn't. My "success" story brought down her defenses and allowed her to imagine future cooperation between gays and lesbians and the police, instead of the more commonplace homophobic failures of the system. If an alliance happened once, it could be repeated.

>

In October 1992, Kevin and I were in Oregon with Donna and Linda at the Lesbian Community Project, located on the third floor of a functioning railway station in downtown Portland. Partitions divided the large room into several work stations, but at five-thirty, they were empty. The center of the room was a comfortable staff lounge where the four of us were going over the upcoming five days of speaking engagements to fight Oregon's Measure 9, including a hearing with the governor's Affirmative Action Office and talks at Portland State University and in Eugene. Every time the heavy wooden door to the office shuddered open, Donna and Linda's eyes darted toward the sound. After the first few times, my shoulders began to jump in time with their glances.

As we discussed press packets and media contacts, I had my first inkling of the level of fear these activists were living with. The relief was almost tangible each time the figure at the door was a woman dropping off materials or stopping in to ask a question. Nevertheless, in the air and in my mind a picture appeared invisibly behind the door: a man holding an automatic weapon, ready to follow the next volunteer in and blow us all away.

I experienced firsthand during the following week why Donna and Linda's nerves were so frayed. It is difficult to assess real versus imagined danger when your organization receives abusive messages and death threats on its answering machine every day. When your friends with *NO ON 9* bumper stickers have cars pull up beside them with drivers who make eye contact and then show a weapon. When gay activists find bullets in their mailboxes attached to slips of paper with their names written on them, sometimes waking later to shots in the night. Kevin and I heard about brakelines sliced and lugnuts loosened. Vandalism and arson. Two women who had their *NO ON 9* sign taken down so many times that they finally posted it on a redwood on their property. The tree was cut down. And most foreboding, the firebombing of an apartment which led to the deaths of Hattie Mae Cohen and Brian Mock, a gay man and a lesbian living together in Salem, Oregon.

Measure 9, Oregon's ballot initiative to amend the state constitution to declare homosexuality abnormal and immoral, had unleashed not just debate, but hate and brutality. The gay and lesbian community and its allies were being terrorized. Statistics collected by the Homophobic Violence Hotline and the *NO ON 9* campaign clearly documented a dramatic rise in antigay attacks since the "debate" began. The violence and threats were continuous, widespread, and anonymous.

The effect of this threatening atmosphere, besides panic in the community as a whole, was to make a normally calm, joyful group of people turn rageful. At Portland State University, one student leader talked about his belief in nonviolence. The young, attractive gay man still believed that peaceful resistance would work in this struggle, despite the hammering the community was taking by the continual harassment and threats. But he also spoke about how members of his group were frustrated and scared and angry. He was unsure he could direct the swelling energy. Would it explode into armed struggle?

Fortunately, the antigay violence did not have the desired effect. The opposition must have hoped to scare the dykes and faggots back underground, to keep us quiet, to make us feel ashamed, make us withdraw from each other so as not to be "guilty" by association. Instead, the community saw that the solution was not to hide. It pulled tighter together, was more out, more loud, more angry, more proud.

We squeaked by in Oregon, 53 to 47 percent, which meant it wasn't just people who were planting bullets in mailboxes or making threatening calls who voted in favor of Measure 9. Three percent is small insurance that our lesbian and gay lives are valuable. In the days surrounding the vote, it was clear that regardless of this particular outcome, education—education as constant and widespread and grassroots as the threats of violence were during the campaign—is crucial to our survival.

I thought about this violence in relationship to the violence I experienced. The point is not which is worse, a sudden, focused explosion or escalating, ubiquitous coercion. The ranking is not useful; the similarity is. The climate in Oregon clarified for me the fear of death with which lesbians and gay men live—all the time. Murder and the threat of murder keep us hidden, quiet, and ashamed. The Oregon community understood this as the violence escalated and the threat became obvious. My community began to feel it the day after I was shot. Each realized it in slightly different ways. While part of Karen may have always been aware that places as seemingly innocuous as highway rest stops are dangerous for a lesbian, until she was en route to Washington, D.C. it had never occurred to her not to get out of the car. In times of crisis the fear of antigay violence emerges out of the recesses where gay and lesbian people usually keep it buried, forced by homophobia into the full light of day.

˒ NINE ˒

On September 24, 1990, the Superior Court of the Harrisburg District denied the defense's appeal on the pretrial motions. Michael George's request on behalf of Stephen Roy Carr to be heard by the Pennsylvania State Supreme Court was denied. The only further recourse was for the case to appear before the U.S. Supreme Court. Since none of the pretrial issues are related to U.S. constitutional law, the possibility of a hearing is highly unlikely. For the rest of his life, Stephen Roy Carr does what he does in a maximum security prison in Pennsylvania.

˒

Activism has been exciting. While helping to lay the educational and political groundwork to combat antigay violence, I have had a number of high-profile adventures. I never imagined being invited to the White House signing ceremony for the Hate Crimes Statistics Act, or influencing the formation of a platform on gay politics with 1992 presidential candidate Ross Perot.

Sometimes it's difficult to accept that these exciting experiences are a by-product of Rebecca's death. I have to remind myself that the fact of her murder is true forever, regardless of how I choose to spend the rest of my life. No amount of reclusiveness, or activism, will bring her back. No amount of misery or rage on my part will change the events of May 13, 1988, or demonstrate my love for her.

I am part of a small minority of victims of trauma who turn to public activism. The vast majority opt to do their personal healing and go on with their lives. While victims may be attractive spokespeople for advocacy groups, public exposure may not be on their personal agenda or the best way to further their healing. I have been able to contribute to public awareness because I had my own timetable for public exposure. If Abbe, Kevin, and my family had not supported—and even insisted on—my timing, I might not have been able to contribute anything. Retaining personal control was invaluable to me. NGLTF was a model victim advocacy organization in that way. They put aside their political agenda, helped me to avoid the revictimization of a quick media fix, and respectfully supported my gradual path toward politics.

The knowledge that I've made a difference and the recognition I get are fuel for my survival and my activism. But they have also brought a sense of isolation. Because of my experiences, people see me as unusual, and sometimes unusual becomes separate and lonely. Political contribution, even by telling a personal story, does not ensure personal connection. I was suddenly catapulted into leadership; I didn't come up through the ranks of gay politics. Who are my peers? Will anyone approach me outside of my survivor role? Can people make the transition to Claudia the architect, the tennis partner? Just because I'm the protagonist of this story, will they allow me to struggle, like they do, with my job, my relationships, my future?

For years I didn't want the pace to stop. Before the stimulation of the case in the courts faded, it was replaced by political activism. While activism was still crescendoing, I pushed myself into a new, extremely demanding architectural job. To keep the pitch high, I even read thriller-mystery novels and watched scary movies.

During one period, about four years after the shooting, life became almost unmanageable. My daily schedule was out of control. I never relaxed, I was starting to sleep poorly, and began having bad dreams again. A new love in Ithaca, which I had great hopes for, floundered. The routine highs and lows of life seemed too flat—I had become a "stimulation junkie." Perhaps Judith Herman's conjecture that trauma survivors get the need for intensity programmed into their bodies applied to me.*

The Post-Traumatic Stress Disorder symptoms had resurfaced in earnest. It is common for survivors to have different aspects of the trauma come up, years after the incident, and get processed over time in a spiral of healing. While I was disappointed that I wasn't completely "well," I also recognized that I needed help and sought out therapy again. My new therapist was brilliant, a feminist, and skilled at treating Post-Traumatic Stress Disorder, as well as issues around death and dying. I gained some insight as the crisis period subsided. The next time the hard part of the spiral comes around, I hope I can keep my perspective and remember that symptoms resurfacing are an indication that more healing is waiting to happen.

Though my recovery demands a lot of attention, I am not alone in the need for healing. The pain of Rebecca's family, while far less visible than mine, has possibly the deepest reach and longest duration. My friends, especially those closest in, have also been traumatized, though no bullets actually pierced their skin. Their healing lagged behind mine in some ways because so many were propelled into caretaking, phone-calling, demonstrating, or were forced to return to their "normal" lives much more quickly than I. As a community, we continue to face the trauma of antigay violence and the loss of our illusion of safety.

We live with an awareness of the continuum of violence. The same forces that encourage harassment of gay people and

---

*Judith Herman, *Trauma and Recovery* (Basic Books, 1992), pp. 38-39.

vandalism of their property also lead people in other circumstances to job and housing discrimination and custody battles, and in other circumstances to assault and murder. Most people are not aware that the continuum stretches all the way to death, but in this community, we are aware. Not only do we remember, we never forget.

None of my close friends from Ithaca or Blacksburg ever go camping or backpacking anymore, as far as I know. As a community, we have sacrificed time in the woods. Even women acquaintances at conferences and women's music festivals have told me that ever since they heard about what happened, they feel less safe in the woods. Some still go, but the nurturing feeling of being with the earth that they used to have has waned.

Still, politically, we forge new trails. We successfully challenged the Pennsylvania Crime Victims Compensation Board's decision to deny payment for expenses incurred in Hershey by "nonblood" family. In Ithaca, we fought for and won both a city and county-wide "fair practices" ordinance, outlawing discrimination based on sexual preference. We have an antihomophobia speakers' bureau, a city domestic partners provision, and are pushing for insurance coverage for same-sex partners. There are over a dozen children who are being raised by two *legal* moms in our community, through adoption, with many others in alternative though not legally recognized families. Despite our increased awareness of risk, we have not compromised lesbian visibility, knowing that to do so is the trap the perpetrators of violence have set.

⸙

While I was in the hospital at Hershey the heavens opened up and it rained torrentially for three days. The police said the campsite was flooded. It felt like the earth was cleansing itself. Unfortunately, the traces of violence are not so easily washed from our minds.

I remember distinctly, as I walked alone on the trail after the shooting, how intensely silent the normal sounds of the forest seemed compared to the gun's explosions. I wondered if the birds were communicating about the horror they had witnessed that afternoon. Though the gunshots have been, for the most part, quieted in my mind, though I have healed from my wounds, though my family and I work to cleanse our lives of the violence, though we speak out widely in the world, as a community we will always walk with an awareness of that silent trail.

, AFTERWORD ,

The world stopped again on Friday, August 12, 1994, when Anne called from where she was vacationing in Colorado with the tragic news that her father and Gina's son Taylor, age five-and-a-half, had been killed in a massive car wreck. We are still facing the reality and pain of this loss. My son Reuben's birth, exactly thirty days later, is a bright spot in this darkness.

"The only measure of your words and your deeds will be the love you leave behind when you're done." ("Everything Possible"/Fred Small/Pine Barrens Music)

· SOURCE NOTES ·

The events described in this book are all true. Many individuals helped to reconstruct the details surrounding the shooting on May 13, 1988, including Anne Rhodes, Satya Rhodes-Conway, Gina Kolb, Karen Poiani, Evelyn Wight, Chris Hays Dove, Andrea Fleck Clardy, Ellen Baer, and Kris Miller. We also used a variety of written and recorded materials, including transcripts, newspaper articles, speeches, diaries, court documents, book articles, and video documentation. All dialogue and descriptions are either taken from one of these sources or have been reconstructed from participants' memories to the best of their abilities.

The errors and omissions are the authors'.

Barringer, Judy. *One Day in Ithaca: May 17, 1988*, Carol Kammen, editor (Ithaca, NY: Ithaca Centennial Press, 1989).

Berrill, Kevin T. and Herek, Gregory M., editors. *Hate Crimes: Confronting Violence Against Lesbians and Gay Men* (Newbury Park, CA: Sage Publications, 1992).

Capote, Truman. *In Cold Blood* (Random House, 1966).

Commonwealth v. Stephen Roy Carr, Court of Common Pleas, Adams County, PA: *Opinion on Post-Verdict Motions*, Oscar Spicer, Presiding Judge

Herman, M.D., Judith Lewis. *Trauma and Recovery: The Aftermath of Violence from Domestic Abuse to Political Terror* (Basic Books, 1992).

Hochman, Anndee. *Everyday Acts & Small Subversions: Women Reinventing Family, Community and Home* (Portland, OR: Eighth Mountain Press, 1994).

National Lesbian and Gay Task Force. *Anti-Gay Violence: Victimization and Defamation in 1988*.

Segrest, Mab. "An Organizer's Memoir" in *Bridges* (Volume 3, Number 1, Spring/Summer 1992).

Smith, Abbe. "Where Angels Fear to Tread: On Representing a Victim of a Crime," forthcoming in *Law Stories*, Gary Bellow and Martha Minnow, editors (Ann Arbor: University of Michigan Press, 1995).

Testing the Limits. Unedited video.

Transcript of testimony at the preliminary hearing held on June 23, 1988 in Courtroom #1 of the Adams County Courthouse, Gettysburg, PA, before Harold R. Deardorff, District Magistrate (Official Court Reporter, Alicia K. Wooters).

Other titles from Firebrand Books include:

Artemis In Echo Park, Poetry by Eloise Klein Healy/$8.95
Before Our Eyes, A Novel by Joan Alden/$8.95
Beneath My Heart, Poetry by Janice Gould/$8.95
The Big Mama Stories by Shay Youngblood/$8.95
The Black Back-Ups, Poetry by Kate Rushin/$9.95
A Burst Of Light, Essays by Audre Lorde/$9.95
Cecile, Stories by Ruthann Robson/$8.95
Crime Against Nature, Poetry by Minnie Bruce Pratt/$8.95
Diamonds Are A Dyke's Best Friend by Yvonne Zipter/$9.95
Dykes To Watch Out For, Cartoons by Alison Bechdel/$8.95
Dykes To Watch Out For: The Sequel, Cartoons by Alison Bechdel/$9.95
Exile In The Promised Land, A Memoir by Marcia Freedman/$8.95
Experimental Love, Poetry by Cheryl Clarke/$8.95
Eye Of A Hurricane, Stories by Ruthann Robson/$8.95
The Fires Of Bride, A Novel by Ellen Galford/$8.95
Food & Spirits, Stories by Beth Brant (*Degonwadonti*)/$8.95
Forty-Three Septembers, Essays by Jewelle Gomez/$10.95
Free Ride, A Novel by Marilyn Gayle/$9.95
A Gathering Of Spirit, A Collection by North American Indian Women
    edited by Beth Brant (*Degonwadonti*)/$10.95
Getting Home Alive by Aurora Levins Morales and Rosario Morales/$9.95
The Gilda Stories, A Novel by Jewelle Gomez/$10.95
Good Enough To Eat, A Novel by Lesléa Newman/$10.95
Humid Pitch, Narrative Poetry by Cheryl Clarke/$8.95
Jewish Women's Call For Peace edited by Rita Falbel, Irena Klepfisz, and
    Donna Nevel/$4.95
Jonestown & Other Madness, Poetry by Pat Parker/$7.95
Just Say Yes, A Novel by Judith McDaniel/$9.95
The Land Of Look Behind, Prose and Poetry by Michelle Cliff/$8.95
Legal Tender, A Mystery by Marion Foster/$9.95
Lesbian (Out)law, Survival Under the Rule of Law by Ruthann Robson/$9.95
A Letter To Harvey Milk, Short Stories by Lesléa Newman/$9.95
Letting In The Night, A Novel by Joan Lindau/$8.95
Living As A Lesbian, Poetry by Cheryl Clarke/$7.95
Metamorphosis, Reflections on Recovery by Judith McDaniel/$7.95
Mohawk Trail by Beth Brant (*Degonwadonti*)/$7.95
Moll Cutpurse, A Novel by Ellen Galford/$7.95
The Monarchs Are Flying, A Novel by Marion Foster/$8.95
More Dykes To Watch Out For, Cartoons by Alison Bechdel/$9.95
Movement In Black, Poetry by Pat Parker/$8.95
My Mama's Dead Squirrel, Lesbian Essays on Southern Culture
    by Mab Segrest/$9.95
New, Improved! Dykes To Watch Out For, Cartoons by Alison Bechdel/$8.95
Normal Sex by Linda Smukler/$8.95
Now Poof She Is Gone, Poetry by Wendy Rose/$8.95

The Other Sappho, A Novel by Ellen Frye/$8.95
Out In The World, International Lesbian Organizing by Shelley Anderson/
$4.95
Politics Of The Heart, A Lesbian Parenting Anthology edited by
Sandra Pollack and Jeanne Vaughn/$12.95
Post-Diagnosis, Poetry by Sandra Steingraber/$9.95
Presenting. . .Sister NoBlues by Hattie Gossett/$8.95
Rebellion, Essays 1980–1991 by Minnie Bruce Pratt/$12.95
Restoring The Color Of Roses by Barrie Jean Borich/$9.95
A Restricted Country by Joan Nestle/$9.95
Running Fiercely Toward A High Thin Sound, A Novel by Judith Katz/$9.95
Sacred Space by Geraldine Hatch Hanon/$9.95
Sanctuary, A Journey by Judith McDaniel/$7.95
Sans Souci, And Other Stories by Dionne Brand/$8.95
Scuttlebutt, A Novel by Jana Williams/$8.95
S/he by Minnie Bruce Pratt/$10.95
Shoulders, A Novel by Georgia Cotrell/$9.95
Simple Songs, Stories by Vickie Sears/$8.95
Sister Safety Pin, A Novel by Lorrie Sprecher/$9.95
Skin: Talking About Sex, Class & Literature by Dorothy Allison/$13.95
Spawn Of Dykes To Watch Out For, Cartoons by Alison Bechdel/$9.95
Speaking Dreams, Science Fiction by Severna Park/$9.95
Stardust Bound, A Novel by Karen Cadora/$8.95
Staying The Distance, A Novel by Franci McMahon/$9.95
Stone Butch Blues, A Novel by Leslie Feinberg/$11.95
The Sun Is Not Merciful, Short Stories by Anna Lee Walters/$8.95
Talking Indian, Reflections on Survival and Writing by Anna Lee Walters/
$10.95
Tender Warriors, A Novel by Rachel Guido deVries/$8.95
This Is About Incest by Margaret Randall/$8.95
The Threshing Floor, Short Stories by Barbara Burford/$7.95
Trash, Stories by Dorothy Allison/$9.95
We Say We Love Each Other, Poetry by Minnie Bruce Pratt/$8.95
The Women Who Hate Me, Poetry by Dorothy Allison/$8.95
Words To The Wise, A Writer's Guide to Feminist and Lesbian Periodicals &
Publishers by Andrea Fleck Clardy/$5.95
The Worry Girl, Stories from a Childhood by Andrea Freud Loewenstein/
$8.95
Yours In Struggle, Three Feminist Perspectives on Anti-Semitism and Racism
by Elly Bulkin, Minnie Bruce Pratt, and Barbara Smith/ $9.95

**You can buy Firebrand titles at your bookstore, or order them directly from
the publisher (141 The Commons, Ithaca, New York 14850, 607-272-0000).
Please include $3.00 shipping for the first book and $.50 for each additional
book.**

A free catalog is available on request.